I0813586

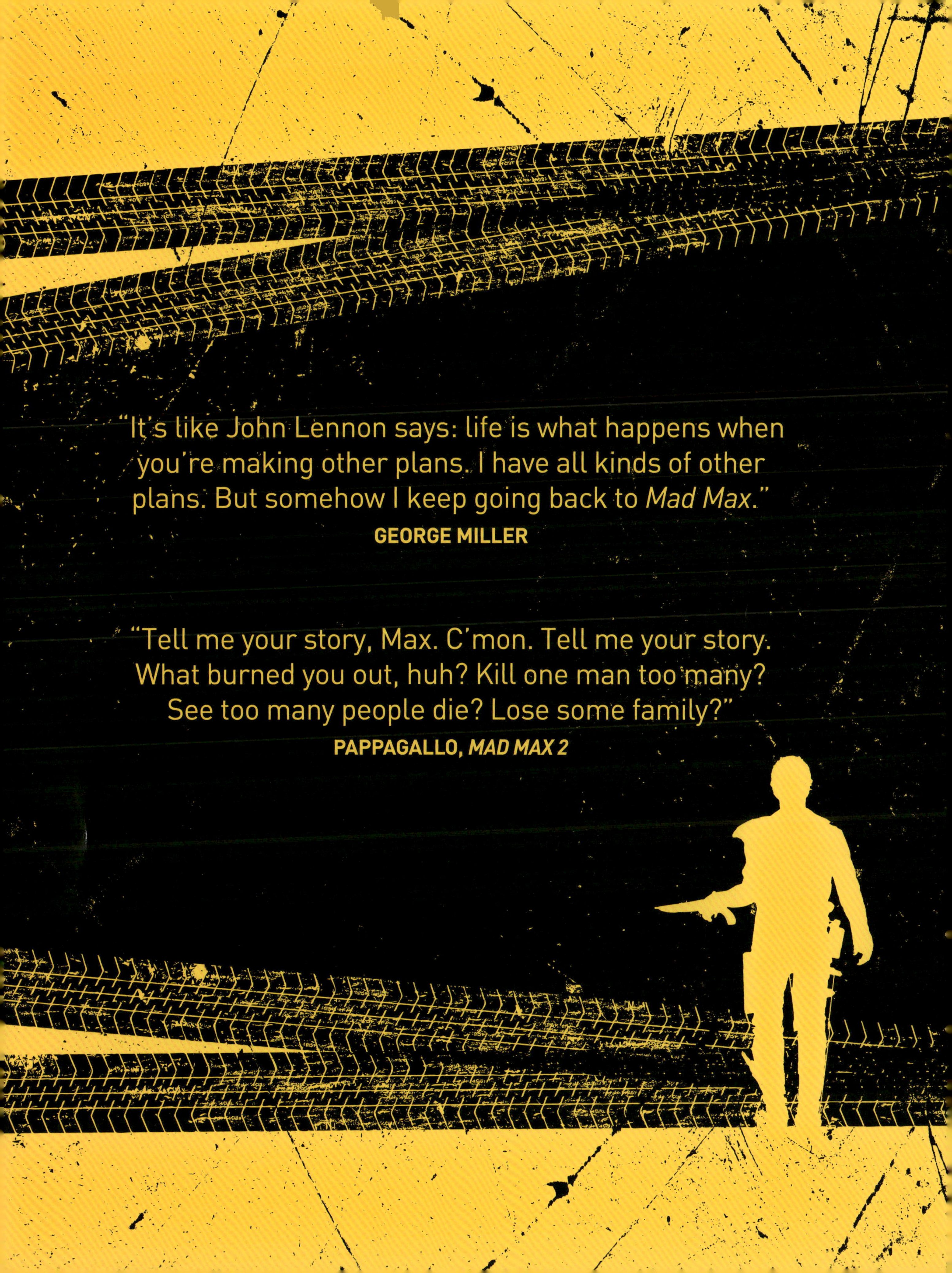
"It's like John Lennon says: life is what happens when you're making other plans. I have all kinds of other plans. But somehow I keep going back to *Mad Max*."
GEORGE MILLER
"Tell me your story, Max. C'mon. Tell me your story. What burned you out, huh? Kill one man too many? See too many people die? Lose some family?"
PAPPAGALLO, *MAD MAX 2*

THE LEGEND OF MAD MAX

IAN NATHAN

PALAZZO

First published in 2024 by Palazzo Editions Ltd
15 Church Road
London, SW13 9HE
www.palazzoeditions.com

We acknowledge the Traditional Owners of the land on which these films were made. We pay our respects to their Elders, past and present, and the Aboriginal Elders of other communities.

A CIP catalogue record for this book is available from the British Library.
Hardback ISBN 9781786751423

Bound and printed in China
10 9 8 7 6 5 4 3 2 1

Designed by Amazing15 for Palazzo Editions

PROLOGUE:

INTERCEPTOR

"ANY LONGER OUT ON THAT ROAD AND I'M ONE OF THEM, YOU KNOW? A TERMINAL CRAZY."

– MAX ROCKATANSKY.

Murray Smith had the Interceptor sat outside his workshop. It was gone to hell: coated in rust and bird shit, a shadow of its former glory. Already battered and bruised after the abuses of a twelve-week shoot and the unforgiving Australian tarmac, the V8 Ford Falcon XB GT Interceptor had been presented to *Mad Max*'s mechanic in lieu of wages owed by a production that was, at that point, flat out of cash. That was 1979, and he would always be able to verify it was the original having scratched his initials inside the driver's door. "I had tried to sell it, for $7,000," he confessed, "and a couple of people came to look at it, but if they had bought it they would be laughing now."

PREVIOUS SPREAD: A Melbourne Force Patrol Ford Falcon "Interceptor" makes its mark on the open highway in the original *Mad Max*. The putative police of the near future are clearly established in ensuing chases by their garish colour scheme. The landscape is still a defined location.

OPPOSITE: A precise copy of the legendary V8 Ford Falcon XB GT Interceptor on show in Silverton, near Broken Hill, New South Wales, where *Mad Max 2* was filmed. This is what you might call the spruced down version for the sequel.

For in 1980 came the demand for a second *Mad Max* film and a second star-turn for what Smith liked to call the "scourge of the highways." An unthinkable outcome after they had scrabbled to get anything coherent in the camera on the first, with the crew left baffled by what whimsical director George Miller and his more outspoken producer Byron Kennedy thought they were making. Frankly, it was a state of chaos. There were serious injuries, and lives were genuinely put at risk. But this wasn't recklessness so much as naivety. They didn't really have much idea how to shoot an action film, but they weren't letting that stop them. He recalled Miller's habit of confronting the numerous problems by standing stock still, eyes closed, tuning out the furies of the set like a man in a trance.

Nevertheless, the Interceptor was pulled out of retirement and given a more rugged look (it was halfway there already) to fit the aesthetic of an even more ambitious – and dangerous – film. Two large fuel tanks bulged out of the boot space, and it was purposely battered to

Silverton
Souvenirs
Open
MAX-079

"IT WAS DESIGNED TO FULFIL THE FANTASIES OF A LARGE CROSS-SECTION OF THE AUDIENCE, TO A DEGREE THAT WOULD SATISFY *US*."

– BYRON KENNEDY

ABOVE: Hollywood inspiration – director George Miller yearned to homage Steve McQueen in *Bullitt*, by appropriating his iconic Mustang GT Fastback in Highland Green for *Mad Max*. Proving beyond their means they had to create their own icon.

ABOVE RIGHT: The streets of San Francisco – the car stunts of *Bullitt* were also a touchstone for Miller. But he was intent on taking automotive thrills to a hyperbolic level. *Mad Max* was a parody of the Hollywood mode.

OPPOSITE: Mel Gibson poses on the bonnet of the Ford Falcon Interceptor – a more punk rock version of screen cool.

resemble the tarnished beauty of the driver, who now supped from cans of dog food and growled his sixteen lines of dialogue (less than Schwarzenegger in *The Terminator*) without feeling, just a nihilistic cant to fit this lone warrior of our perilous future.

The story of the car is the story of the films and the story of the man. The Interceptor is an extension of Max Rockatansky. Vengeance on wheels, black-on-black, whiplash bursts of nitro-fuelled acceleration: an icon transformed as the further adventures of *Mad Max* transformed the hero and scorched the world beneath him. "Cars are a metaphor for power," said Colin Gibson, production designer on *Fury Road*, who was set the Herculean task of launching another fleet of hare-brained muscle cars, gas-guzzling potpourris of spare parts, and relaunching Max's Interceptor with a Tom Hardy-shaped Max as the one not-so-careful owner. He's right, cars are power in Miller's dystopian wasteland. But they represent freedom too. And religious artefacts of what has come before.

"It was designed to fulfil the fantasies of a large cross-section of the audience," explained Byron Kennedy back in 1979, "to a degree that would satisfy *us*." The producer was largely responsible for the look of the "Black on Black," as he christened it, after the two layers of paint, gloss over matt. They made the car that they wanted to see on a cinema screen.

He and Miller had set their hearts on a Mustang GT Fastback like the Highland Green 1968 model Steve McQueen drove in *Bullitt*, as modified by the former racing car driver turned stuntman who went by the name of *Max Balchowksy*. They had set aside $20,000 for their star vehicle, a paltry sum by any standards, and the Mustang had to be rationalised to three white 1973 V8 Ford Falcon XB GT Interceptors bought from Rural Motors, Orange, in New South Wales. Two were used for the canary yellow cop cars and would perish in the line of duty.

The original Interceptor model was born out of the Australian enthusiasm for muscle car tour racing at tracks like Bathurst and Sandhurst. Curves were everything, streamlining metal; this was the end of the "Coke bottle" era of design. The last one would roll off the assembly line a month before the original *Mad Max* was released. To Kennedy's specifications, the Fords were modified for near future Melbourne by car customisers Graf-X, with the hero vehicle

gaining a dual coat of black paint, extended fibreglass nose, rear spoiler, souped-up V8 engine and twin Weiand superchargers lifted from a dragster that poked up through the bonnet like a horn, although not technically attached to the engine but rather a battery-powered prop. It was Kennedy who drove it onto set for the first time, throttling the engine, making it growl. Miller grinned. "Wow," was all he could say. It was Kennedy who made sure it remained immaculate throughout.

In the first film, the Interceptor is gifted to Mel Gibson's Max, his youthful blue eyes already brimming with demons, by the Main Force Patrol, the underfunded remnants of Melbourne's federal police, desperately trying to keep order on the roads as society begins to fragment. Max tries to walk away, tired of the violence, the risk, the line between good and bad beginning to blur. "Any longer out on that road and I'm one of them, you know? A terminal crazy," he pleads. But an unspeakable act of violence against him, the murder of his wife and child by a deranged biker gang, will strip away his humanity, turning him into the killing machine he feared he would become. The Interceptor will be his weapon and the fulcrum of his madness.

"It was an intimidation thing," appreciated Phil Brock, Gibson's stunt driver, the *other* Max who pushed the Interceptor through 100 mph on the Melbourne backroads. Brock and his brother Peter, sons of a bush mechanic, had raced in the Bathhurst 1000. In the seventies, Phil was considered the best stunt driver in Australia, the king of precision steering. On set, Miller would explain what he wanted the car to do, and Brock and his fellow drivers would have to figure out how to do it. "We had to improvise on the spot," he said, drawing inspiration from Spielberg's *Duel*, which had pitched a Plymouth Reliant against a 1961 Peterbilt 281 monster truck in the Californian desert. Such were the limited

resources available to the production, the Interceptor would also be used to transport cast, crew and materials to set.

Mad Max began as a dream – a challenge between two friends, one posing as a fast-talking producer, while the other was supposed to be a doctor not a director. They were in their twenties and fitted one another like a double-act: Kennedy and Miller, sense and sensibility, motion and poetry. Though it could as easily be the other way around. The standard legend has Miller as the thoughtful one and Kennedy the mouthpiece, but on that first film, amid the chaos, the producer would often be spotted sat behind the wheel of the Interceptor making *vroom-vroom* noises like a child, living in this supercharged world.

They were equally determined to do things their way. Which was a joke. They were bereft of know-how, making it up as they went along, punk rockers standing at the gates of an opera house. That was key. As with that disruptive wunderkind Orson Welles (he too was in his twenties when he shook up the world, albeit with slightly different subject matter), if you don't know the rules how can you stick to them? *Mad Max* had no speed limit. And on a budget of $350,000, which meant cutting corners in every sense, a sum raised through private donations (a grand Kennedy scheme to bypass studio control), their little, home-grown action film made $100 million in three years. Until *The Blair Witch Project* in 1999, the most profitable movie of all time.

This was about chemistry, desire, passion and that ineffable catalyst known as destiny. And it is about drive in every sense. There was something in Miller's imagination, like a prodigious musical gift. He could sense a film, feel it beneath his skin. It was a matter of reaching for it. Straining for it. Each of the five interlinked yet individual films that take up the continuing *Mad Max* saga have nearly destroyed him. And it was his crucial relationship with Kennedy, cut tragically short after *Mad Max 2*, that gave voice to his visual rock 'n' roll.

They were junkies for American movies, but Australian blood ran through their veins. *Mad Max* is such an Australian film: the outback twang of its dialogue, anti-authoritarian barbs, and doomsday bleakness of its setting.

The call came for more. Max demanded to be heard. Set incrementally further into an atavistic future, amid a now definitive iconography of S&M maniacs roaring about the nuke-stripped desert in jerry-built roadsters, petrol the new gold, *Mad Max 2* (released as *The Road Warrior* in the United States) set the seal on the original's promise. It is counted as one of the medium's seminal moments, a car chase movie taking chaos into the sublime, and the first to roll the Interceptor.

That wasn't the original, which was only used for close-ups of Gibson at the wheel, making gear changes like thrusts of a knife. An equivalent 1974 Ford Fairmont GS XB arrived in canary yellow to be sprayed black as night as the stunt car for the wide shots and it would come to a dramatic end at the hands of hockey-masked Lord Humungus's road-raging gang, rolling side-over-side, with a bloodied Max crawling out, his face as pummelled as his car. When one of Humungus's over-eager marauders triggers the Interceptor's booby-trapped tank, the stunt car went up in a plume of orange flames. The charred carcass of the Fairmont Interceptor was left among the rocks at Broken Hill in New South Wales like the bones of a metallic dinosaur, until it was scavenged by a mystery collector and hoarded in secret, still to this day.

The original Interceptor, two films down and on its way to being one of the most famous cars in movie history, passed like Black Beauty

ABOVE RIGHT: An MFP Interceptor skids to a halt in *Mad Max* – each day director Miller would explain to his stunt drivers what he required, and they would have to figure out how to make it work. The stunts were often close to being a direct copy of the fiction.

OPPOSITE: Mel Gibson poses on set of *Mad Max 2*. The giveaway that this is a behind-the-scenes shot? The fact that Max is smiling.

between uncaring owners. Eventually, it fell into the hands of Ray Collins and sat forgotten outside his scrapyard until an enterprising collector named Bob Kulinko offered to take it off his hands. Kulinko planned to show it as part of a travelling exhibition in America, spending $25,000 to restore it to the polish of the first *Mad Max*, though he kept the two rear fuel tanks from *Mad Max 2*. Spotting his signature, Murray Smith verified it as the genuine article.

By 1985, *Mad Max* also lay beneath the yoke of American ownership. Hollywood-backed, the narratively emboldened third, *Mad Max Beyond Thunderdome* (to fans: *Thunderdome*), is better than you remember, but threatened Max's nihilistic headspace with a sentimental vein, when he is called upon to save a tribe of abandoned children. We feel the absence when

OPPOSITE: George Miller and producer Doug Mitchell confer on the set of *Fury Road*. Depending on the time of day, the Namib Desert could offer equal parts sweltering heat and biting cold.

BELOW: mayhem is unleashed for the finale of *Mad Max Beyond Thunderdome*. The truck launched skywards is Max's revived Camel Wagon. Secreted under there somewhere is the frame of his old Interceptor.

there is no Interceptor to be found among the array of vehicles that emerge like insects from a nest for the exuberant final act. Gibson's Max begins the film piloting his Camel Wagon across the desert, smothered in a black head-dress like *Lawrence of Arabia*'s evil twin. They were sequels and yet not sequels. A fourth, *Mad Max: Fury Road* (to fans: just *Fury Road*), with a budget a thousand times greater than the original, might be the greatest action movie ever made. In 2012, Max looked like Hardy, but the car remained the same.

It's a saga inside and out: that of Max and Miller (and Kennedy) and of the possibility of action cinema, hurling metal about for real, the poetry of motion and the poetry of arrested motion. These were always films about cars. About *this* car. In the vast mythology that Miller constructed around the fourth film, what he called "Wasteland logic," for years Max had been scavenging the outposts of humanity for parts in order to rebuild the Interceptor, his spirit animal. Indeed he had been interrupted in his quest by the events of *Thunderdome*; in the third film's original script it was hinted that he was using his wagon to transport car parts: mufflers and piping stowed among his dromedaries. Look closely at the Camel Wagon and you'll discern the cab of a Ford Falcon fused to the main chassis.

In the extended universe of the *Fury Road* comics, Max had resurrected his Interceptor two years before the fourth film's opening scene. But things have gotten worse. Max is as damaged as his ride: front fender gone, chrome stripped, scabbed in orange

rust, a busted left headlight (in the shape of Australia). He is planning to light out for the Plains of Silence, a journey from which he and his car will never return.

"It's literally the very first panel of the storyboards, where he's just in the Wasteland, looking out," recalled screenwriter Nico Lathouris. "He wants to get across the Plains of Silence. People have crossed them, but nobody's ever come back." For Lathouris the Plains were a metaphor for a suicidal wish. Max wants to silence the voices in his head.

On the first day of *Fury Road* they totalled the Interceptor again. The sun-scalded winter's day of 2 June 2012 had felt like it would never come. Thirty years of pre-production. This is the opening scene of the movie, which will (brief interiors aside) shoot in chronological order among the furies of the Namib Desert on the southwestern coast of Africa. It is a typical Miller move: a grand symbolic gesture, destroying the spectre of the original Gibson films as Max's famous car is chased by another tribe of road hoodlums hollering like maniacs. Barely one minute twenty-four seconds into the movie, the vehicle flips and rolls, spinning over and over, before skidding on its roof in a cloud of angry dust. There was no way Miller was going to fake it with CGI – you start as you mean to go on. At the wheel is the fifty-four-year-old Guy Norris, who had served as Gibson's stunt driver on *Mad Max 2*.

It was in his blood – the madness. As a teenager Norris had toured town-to-town across Australia with "thrill shows" wowing the locals with medleys of death-defying stunts, things you might see in movies: cowboys falling from second-storey windows, clowns blown sky-high from exploding dunnies, motorcycles leaping through walls of flame. If they raised enough cash, they would smash cars into one another. Safety was secondary. "We thought we were bulletproof," he laughed. The only thing worse than risking your life was not risking your life. *Mad Max 2* was his first gig as a stuntman. He was twenty-one. He must have leaped on that tanker a dozen times. As well as Max, he doubled as Bearclaw Mohawk. That was Norris catapulted from a motorbike and rotating through the air like a tomahawk. In the thirty-two years since *Mad Max 2*, he had watched disdainfully as cinema went soft with the plastic unreality of CGI. Where was the peril? Where was the reality?

"THESE WERE ALWAYS FILMS ABOUT CARS. ABOUT *THIS* CAR ..."

Fury Road was, Norris said, like coming "full circle." After this he could retire. Miller had promised that *Mad Max* was still to be an opera of old-school practical effects. Only now, noted Norris, stunting was more a "collaborative science" involving every department. The safety measures were markedly better than in 1980. Not that it is exactly safe to be rolling a V8

ABOVE: *Fury Road* – Tom Hardy's Max, attempting to escape from the War Boys, finds his precious Interceptor being dismantled ready to be reassembled. For George Miller this was a metaphor for the whole film. Rebuilding the old icons, madder than ever.

across the desert floor, generating centrifugal forces beyond those of a fighter jet. His team wonder if it was really wise for the head of stunts to be inside a crashing car on the very first day of a six-month shoot. Not that anyone is going to talk him out of it.

"I remember going and sitting in the Black on Black and my memory flashed back close to forty years," he said. "And it felt exactly the same."

From those first, silent days, movies thrived on stunts. Teams of stuntmen and women willing to risk their necks to fake a story's thrills by doing them for real. But there was a particular obsession that came with *Mad Max*, born out of the devil-may-care pursuits of that first film, an urge to dare the most reckless stunts in the name of story, marrying speed and camerawork, meeting the call of this deranged mythology. To live the films in their wild glory. Even after all these years, it was the defining motivation. Do it for real.

The on-set mechanics are concerned about the Interceptor's brake line, but Norris doesn't care. Amid a swarm of pursuit vehicles and dirt-bikes, he isn't going to be using the brakes. The supercharged Ford will engage a flipper at sixty miles an hour – basically, a pneumatic paddle attached to the bottom of the car that would set it spinning side-over-side like a toy. Full circle indeed. The latest version of the Interceptor came with its own story. This Falcon V8 was one of three bought from collectors in 2001 for the Gibson variation of *Fury Road*, retrofitted along the lines of *Mad Max 2*, and shipped to Namibia before the film collapsed six weeks before production in 2003. It had found its way back to Australia and a 2007 TV commercial and then languished outside action mechanic Cameron

Manewell's workshop in Villawood, Sydney, until he, by chance, was hired for the Hardy variation of *Fury Road* in 2011. Full circle. When Miller announced *Fury Road*'s rebirth to the press, the Interceptor was there to take a bow.

Gravity and attrition and the hard Namibian earth eventually bring the car to a halt. Inside, wedged in a roll cage, it is as if time slowed. Norris's entire world has become pure sensation, or as he recalled later, like "being in the middle of a washing machine." The first take is magnificent: nine-and-a-half rolls captured on camera. Though in rehearsal, he had managed thirteen rotations – a world record. Norris emerges dazed but intact. *Fury Road* is off to the races.

The lunatic War Boys will lay claim to the wreckage, resurrecting the Interceptor as a wacko dragster renamed Razor Cola, stripped down to the chrome and jacked-up on off-road tyres, with barbwire headlight covers for a more "menacing" look. Two were built for the production by Manewell from two more Ford Falcon coupés. In the *sturm und drang* of *Fury Road*'s finale, the Razor Cola meets its end crushed between Furiosa's War Rig and The People Eater's pantechnicon, flipping, before being consumed in a ball of flame. The remaining Razor Cola stood resplendent before Sydney Opera House for the *Fury Road* premiere.

The original Interceptor was passing into legend. From assembly line to museum piece. An artefact of the future on display in the National Motor Museum of South Australia. That was until 1993, when Peter Nelson shipped it to the UK and the Cars and Stars Motor Museum in Cumbria, where it sat, somewhat absurdly, alongside five of 007's Aston Martins, a few Batmobiles and Chitty Chitty Bang Bang. That was until 2011, when the museum closed, and the collection passed to real estate billionaire Michael Dezer, proprietor of the Miami Auto Museum, before being rehoused again in his Orlando Auto Museum, all shiny and chrome.

In 2021, a fifth film, *Furiosa*, set itself the task of telling a tale of the Wasteland without Max at the wheel. So why is it images leaked from the set of the Interceptor perched, black as a crow, on top of a sandy rise?

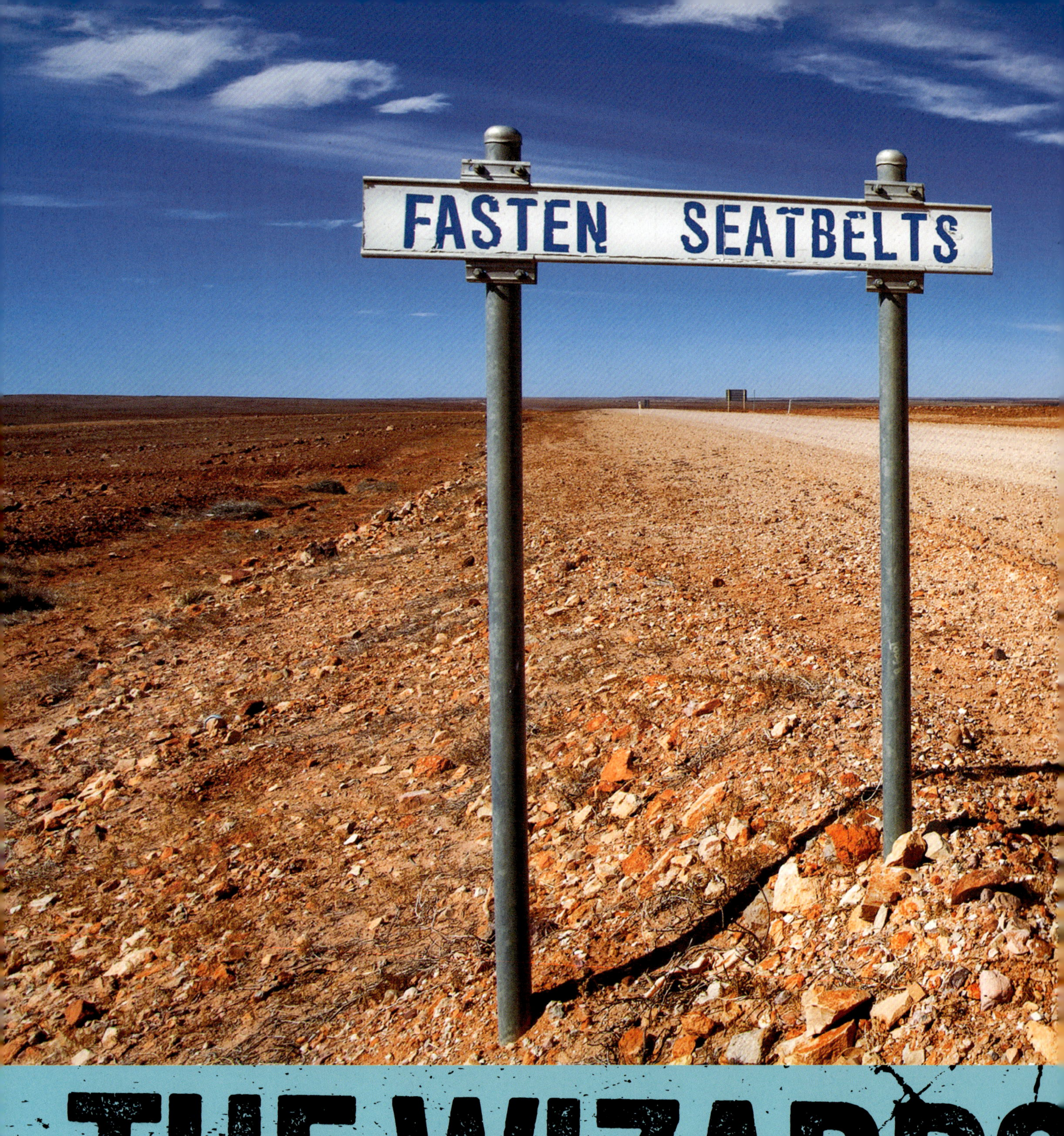

THE WIZARDS

OF OZ

"THERE IS A CULTURE OF VIOLENCE IN OUR COUNTRY."

– GEORGE MILLER

The highways stretched into eternity. Mile upon mile of unbending, sand-dusted asphalt, like an image from a film noir. The couple fleeing through an indifferent desert. The vanishing point of the Yellow Brick Road in Oz. In this parched corner of Southern Queensland, the land is as flat as a salt lake. Barely one-street long, Chinchilla was founded when the railway spread its iron limb westward from the Darling Downs in 1877. The name was derived from *jinchilla*, the Aboriginal word for the Cypress Trees that offered some relief from the sun. Brisbane and civilisation were almost two hundred miles away.

PREVIOUS SPREAD: At its heart, the *Mad Max* saga is about the confrontation between humankind and the vast Australian landscape. Where the blue sky meets the endless horizon. And the laws of the road were already fairly flexible.

OPPOSITE: George Miller lines up a shot on the set of *Fury Road*. From the very beginning, Miller was intent on achieving a form of visual rock'n'roll where the rhythm of images comes close to music.

On 3 March 1945, a population of around two thousand (who was counting?) was swelled by two – twins George and John were born. Their parents, the Millers, Jim and Angela, were formerly the Milotis, Dimitri and Envangalia: first-generation Greek immigrants adapting their identities to the vernacular of a new continent. Their blue-and-white weatherboard house was buoyed by Greek traditions and Greek hospitality. Maybe Greek myths ran in the blood; Homer's embattled heroes testing the fates. Remove the glistening Mediterranean and Chinchilla was the image of Kythera, the Greek island from which the nine-year-old Dimitri waved goodbye to his mother, never to see her again. He and his wife ran Chinchilla's café, serving sundaes and soda, as well as fish delicacies. Where the town gathered to tell their tall tales.

George and John were dizygotic twins, alike but not identical. For one thing, John had blue eyes, and George had plain old brown. They spent virtually the first twenty-two years of their lives together, through school and university. Every day comparing notes. Telling their tales.

TX
Nikon

OPPOSITE: George Miller often cites the formative day when as a young man he took in a double-bill of Gillo Pontecorvo's powerful docudrama *The Battle of Algiers* ...

BELOW: ... and Robert Altman's Vietnam satire (in the guise of Korea) *M*A*S*H*, with the sardonic duo Donald Sutherland and Elliot Gould. The mix of hyper-realistic action with ironic humour would become essential to the Miller style.

John was always funnier, always more interesting. Being a twin taught George Miller what it was to be a storyteller: "The ones that had that extra flavour, that extra surprise, the ones that weren't the sort of standard that you've heard so often before, are the ones that stick in the mind."

Miller looks upon his childhood as idyllic. There were no demons to be slain in his art. No inciting incident to stoke the flames of dystopia. Kids got up to no good until the sun set. A directing career begins the moment you start pretending and have your three brothers (their ranks swelled with siblings Chris and Bill) pretend along with you. George was quiet, in his own head much of the time, but it was he who planned their escapades. Too young to buy a ticket, it was George's idea to hide underneath the floorboards of the Star Theatre, Chinchilla's only cinema, where they could hear the dialogue, the gunshots and the squeal of a getaway car, picturing the images in their heads.

Is this when films began to infiltrate his dreams?

Like all those directors drawn to the flame of genre, he subsisted on comic books, westerns, war stories and fairy tales. All those serial adventures with their solitary heroes. Once old enough to set eyes on them, he became a "typical film freak." Recreating what he had seen in "elaborate games," dressing up as the characters, mounting jousting competitions like the Knights of the Round Table. He was fascinated by action. The doing over the saying.

The Millers moved to Sydney when George was a teen, but the "great long roadways" of Chinchilla were fixed in his mind's eye. The knowledge that beyond the low horizon with its sullen heat haze, the world was stripped bare of houses and shops, cinemas and restaurants, and a vast emptiness lay in wait. In Australia, you were always on the edge of things.

Miller had no idea he wanted to be a filmmaker, but he became increasingly aware he would never be as good a doctor as John. They attended medical school together at the University of New South Wales. But he became distracted. Culture sang from every noticeboard. Theatre, art, music, architecture and cinema in abundance. He began to think differently. He was more passionate. He felt a restlessness to create like a needle pressed against his skin. An artistic streak first took shape as portrait painting, including a series on dancers commissioned by the Australian Ballet. Years from then, with the release of *Mad Max 2*, *The New York Times* would declare Miller "the Diaghilev of demolition derbies."

He was not swayed from his path. If ever he missed a class, his diligent brother would supply the notes. History tells us that Miller became a doctor: mild-mannered, intelligent and dedicated, to a point. But city life awakened new appetites and stirred old dreams. A man on horseback, dressed in black, rides through a desert landscape that finally swallows him up.

Miller would later classify films as "public dreams."

He became a filmmaker in slow motion. It was a chain reaction of epiphanies. He loves to cite the day when, skipping class, he walked through Sydney and came to a cinema. Robert Altman's *M*A*S*H* was the main attraction. Vietnam refracted through the Korean War. Satirical, rowdy, subversion under the cover of slapstick. There was no way he could simply return to class after that. He was buzzing. So he found another cinema, an arthouse. Which was offering Gillo Pontecorvo's *The Battle of Algiers*. Iconic, revolutionary, action as biting as a sandstorm. Days like that will change your life.

> **"[STORIES] THAT HAD THAT EXTRA FLAVOUR, THAT EXTRA SURPRISE ... ARE THE ONES THAT STICK IN THE MIND."**
>
> – GEORGE MILLER

Or the time his brother Chris told him about a competition being mounted by the university's film department. Shoot and edit a one-minute short film in an hour. The lucky winner would be invited to join a workshop in Melbourne for a crash course in film production. Director Peter Weir happened to be one of the judges. The first of the family to see filmmaking as a potential career, Chris enrolled his older brother in his ironic concept (eventually shown on Australian

"WHAT'S SO WRONG ABOUT MOVIES IS THAT THEY'RE NOT REAL."

television). A slow tracking shot approaches a man with long hair, coat and hat from behind. He turns toward camera. The scene cuts to a caption: "What's so wrong about movies is that they're not real." With that, hat, coat, and indeed hair fall to the ground. Nobody was there at all. The simplicity of the idea won the day. Everyone else, said Miller, "tried to make something as big as *Ben-Hur*."

As the nominal director, his brother was officially the recipient of the prize, but Miller wasn't about to let that stop him – he had caught the filmmaking bug – and talked his way onto the workshop. Two significant catalysts were about to redefine the future.

ABOVE: The unlikely maestro – the quietly spoken doctor-turned-director George Miller would prove to have an almost subliminal gift for composing action sequences in his head. Matching them was the challenge.

OPPOSITE: Producer Byron Kennedy, posing as the big-time, two-phone Hollywood guy. In truth, Kennedy was a remarkable mix of canny financial fixer and visionary. He would contribute huge amounts to the story and look of the first two *Mad Max* films.

The first was technical. It wasn't the cameras, the lights, or positioning the actors on a set that were a revelation to Miller. It was the concept of the edit. He had never thought about film in this way. How it manipulated time. "I suddenly saw – oh my God, there is the fourth dimension," he said. This was the defining characteristic of filmmaking. Time travel. That's what gave you narrative. Any aspirations he had to paint were engulfed by the flow (the surge!) of storytelling. The potential to create movement in time and space. To accelerate life. "So it became basically kinetic pictures that I was mainly interested in," he said.

He wanted to create visual rock 'n' roll.

That's when he got chatting to a guy named Byron Kennedy.

From the moment he could talk it was as if Byron wanted to know everything. How does an engine work? How far is it to the Sun? When the doors of the crowded Melbourne department store elevator closed where did they go? "He was like a human question mark," observed his father, Patrick, whose own father had been at Gallipoli, that great Australian misadventure in World War I. Patrick had served in the Royal Australian Air Force during World War II, the kind of man to build their first family home in Yarraville, a working-class suburb of West Melbourne.

Byron arrived into the world on 18 August 1949, with a sense of purpose, and heedless, his mother, Lorna, would have told you, of risk. "He was always running. Always talking. Always playing," she remembered. She named him after the romantic poet.

How he loved speed. When Byron, with pepper-black hair and a sly smile, got his first tricycle, aged three, he was mesmerised by its spinning wheels, pedalling as hard as he could. His grandfather on his mother's side had raced motorcycles across Australia in his youth. The young Byron made sure to capture his tales on his tape recorder so he could listen in again later.

The young Kennedy had a sadistic streak, as his younger sister would attest, being the victim of most of his pranks, pricking her with needles, waking her up with a brief dab from a hot iron. It was Kennedy who was the source of *Mad Max*'s irreverent, macabre spirit. He may have been on the side of the leering, leather-clad gangs. "This guy's humour is really weird," recalled Graham "Grace" Walker, production designer on *Mad Max 2*.

Engines intrigued Kennedy. He restored a go-kart, stripping it down to its essential parts, what made it go. He would view film in a similar way. If you grasped what made it work, you could make it go faster. His fascination with his first Super 8 camera was as much about how it worked as what stories it could tell. Less of a dreamer than Miller, perhaps, he experimented with shots of moving vehicles and planes skimming the horizon at local air shows. He wanted to capture momentum. To decode the relationship between speeding car and stationary ground. Using stop-motion effects to animate toy soldiers, he made a war movie

BELOW: Two babes of the august Australian New Wave, against which George Mille reacted. Here, Fred Schepisi's Aboriginal drama *The Chant of Jimmie Blacksmith* ...

OPPOSITE: ... and here, Gillian Armstrong's tale of female independence *My Beautiful Career*, starring Judy Davis, who was in Mel Gibson's class at drama school.

in his garage called *Battle Cry*. By eighteen, he had founded his own production company, Warlok Films. In his twenties, he was serving as cinematographer, actor, editor, and directing industrial documentaries.

All this would translate into a remarkable, almost paradoxical producer: possessed of both a hard-nosed business sense and an unquenchable sense of filmmaking adventure. Why not attach an actual rocket to a Ford Sedan on a Melbourne highway?

The momentous meeting with Miller arrived without fanfare. Attending that same film workshop, the go-getting-multi-hyphenate-producer-in-the-making got talking to the quiet proto-director and they found they understood one another straightaway. Whatever chemistry might be, they had it. It was filmmaking love at first sight. A perfect fit of personality to personality like gears meshing. Spiritual twins. Miller talked about the possibilities of story; Kennedy measured his tales in practical terms: how they would pull it off, what it might cost, who might want to see what they made?

Miller moved into the Kennedy family home in Melbourne, an extra son at the table. For the young filmmakers it was a way of saving money and beneath the same roof planning a movie, as Kennedy declared, "to set fire to the Australian film industry."

Some context. In the early seventies, assisted by a government fund, a fashion emerged for exceptionally well-made period pieces that capitalised on the country's yawning vistas, infused with the experimental yearnings of a new generation of filmmaker. This was the Australian New Wave. Artists of the calibre of Peter Weir, Philip Noyce, Gillian Armstrong, Bruce Beresford and Fred Schepisi arose from its ranks – all of whom would set sail for Hollywood. There were classics of world cinema among their number: Weir's *Picnic at Hanging Rock*, Beresford's *Breaker Morant*, Armstrong's *My Brilliant Career*, and Schepisi's *The Chant of Jimmie Blacksmith*. A surge of creativity rippled out from Sydney. From virtually nothing over

four hundred films were made over the next decade and a half.

As far as Miller was concerned, the obsession with period was about trying to lay down cultural roots that didn't really exist. "They're too slow," he moaned. They often lacked a hard narrative line or visual style. There was an elitism at work; films that considered themselves art. Retrospectively, Miller's name (and Max's) is often added to the list of New Wave inductees. That, he insisted, was purely circumstantial: "The one link I have with these other people is that we all got started at the same time." That said, he had their boldness, the same sense of experimentation. The same urge, come what may, to get films made.

But Miller and Kennedy were going to make a movie that stripped the veneer from all that art. A jab in the eye of the New Wave. Miller maintained it was as if *Mad Max* had "popped out" from his unconscious. He is also a great one for post-rationalisation – following the thread back out of the maze. And they were certainly panhandling for a real taste of their homeland: jagged and wild, and fast. The subject matter, he said, sprang directly out of the things he grew up with.

"If you look back and try to pick up the origins of something, there is a cult of violence in our country, with tons of accidents on the roads which we all seem to accept quite blithely. . ." As Americans have gun culture, he explained, "we have a car culture." This was an Australian reflex – to satirise a homegrown, gung-ho attitude with the same lick of energy, the same goonish idea of machismo, and a spin on the hybrid slang that had formed as colonial whites fused working-class English with the singsong tribal dialects of the Aboriginal people.

Out in the sticks, out in a town like Chinchilla, car culture was a socially acceptable form of violence. Fender-benders, pile-ups, high-speed collisions. That was the wellspring for Max. Miller had experienced it first-hand: "I lost three friends in accidents, when they were teenagers." It was an extension of the leathery, survivalist bravado of the European settlers, with their convict DNA, faced with this arid slab at the end of the world. At its heart, *Mad Max* is a confrontation between humankind and a hostile environment.

Miller wasn't a petrolhead. He liked cars well enough, had his tales from those idle, teenaged nights haring through Chinchilla. But he had no insight into engines, torque, camshafts and fuel injection. Models were judged purely on aesthetics. He didn't talk the talk. That was all Kennedy. He thought the thought.

There was always that thesis being written in the back of Miller's head. He was always one step ahead of the critics. His very first film, back in 1971, the very first film on which he and Kennedy began egging each other on, was a twenty-minute short tartly entitled *Violence in Cinema Part 1*. It was both provocation and premonition, as well as absurdist film analysis, in which a mock psychologist called Dr. Fyne (Arthur Dignam) discusses violence in cinema, before an outbreak of that very violence interrupts his lecture. Miller was getting ahead

of the nihilism to come with Max, all the calls to have his road movie banned. A media storm brewing on the horizon.

"The mass audience has always demanded a heavy saturation of violence," gurns Dr. Fyne. He cites the Bond movies, *Bonnie and Clyde* and *The Wild Bunch*. Mainstream violence. American violence. *Mad Max* was taking a road as old as the hills.

When *Violence in Cinema Part 1* got picked up for distribution (playing before the main attractions), Kennedy and Miller decided the time had come to make their feature film. This was around 1973 to 1974, when Max took the unlikely form of a crusading journalist. Miller had heard about a local radio reporter who specialised in interviewing the survivors of car crashes. It was an ignoble enterprise. The hack was feeding on our voyeuristic urges, but it resonated with Miller's feelings about working in casualty. How the doctors processed death so causally. Otherwise you went mad.

What is obvious, certainly to Miller, is that *Mad Max* would never have been born without the sobering nights on the emergency ward at St. Vincent's Hospital in Sydney, where he served as a resident. Medicine taught you about the human condition in a visceral way. There was a night when five people were rushed into the ER, victims of another car accident. A young girl ended up before Miller, wrapped in a rubber blanket. Lifting it, he could see there was little left of her legs. He struggled to find a vein for the IV, finally inserting it in her neck. She was conscious throughout. "Die me. Die me. Die me," she whimpered. She wouldn't make it through the night.

"Obviously, when you're practising medicine you are seeing at least the aftermath of violence a lot more than you normally would," he said. "Hospitals are like little clearing houses of pathology and trauma."

"THE MASS AUDIENCE HAS ALWAYS DEMANDED A HEAVY SATURATION OF VIOLENCE."

– DR. FYNE

There was a period when Miller set himself up as an emergency locum service in Melbourne, with Kennedy at the wheel of his ramshackle Mazda Bongo, hurtling through the night from victim to victim. Things you never forgot. Real experiences. But they still managed to go home and sleep.

Miller would never have become a filmmaker if he hadn't been a doctor. He had meant to go back to medicine, until in the mid-eighties he realised he just didn't have the time. But he would always see the parallels: "First of all, it's all about point of view. As a doctor, you're looking at the complete human being, down a microscope or on an X-ray or as part of a

OPPOSITE: In his first film made alongside Byron Kennedy, the parodic short *Violence in Cinema Part 1*, George Miller has a fake academic disapproving of hyper-violent classics such as, here, *The Wild Bunch* ...

ABOVE: ... and, here, Faye Dunaway and Warren Beatty in *Bonnie and Clyde*, a film which hares along long, flat highways. The irony being that they are two films that served as great inspiration for *Mad Max*.

collective. Viscerally, intellectually, spiritually, anthropologically. And then, on a practical level, it's invaluable. The first night-shoot reminded me of night sessions on emergency. Problem solving. Thinking on your feet. Never knowing what was coming through the door."

Miller soon realised that a desensitised journalist wasn't nearly as cinematic as a desensitised cop. Ideas began to flow. How would that cop react if something happened to his own family? If it got personal? A story took shape around a young Melbourne police officer who can no longer keep the madness at bay when his wife and child are killed by a roving biker gang. A tale of vengeance emerged, a western on wheels. "I know we wanted a cop going berserk," recalled Miller. With Kennedy's eager input, they unashamedly planned to propel their hero down the highways of the city following the impulse of the car chase. But with a new mania all their own.

The repeated traumas of the ER had a paradoxical effect on Miller as filmmaker. Rather than aversion, he was drawn to images of wrecked cars, metal thrown against metal, carnage on the open road. Less the Ballardian provocation of *Crash* (directed by another placid former science student in David Cronenberg), Miller translated his searing memories into a kinetic energy and violence on the edge of the real world. Maybe it was a form of catharsis. It was certainly visual rock 'n' roll. But not without a moral dimension. The repercussions of crash culture send tremors through *Mad Max*. Max's descent into madness begins with the sight of fellow cop Goose's burned-up body.

The problem was the more scenes Miller came up with, the more absurd the story seemed when applied to a contemporary world. "It was just too hyperbolic," he said.

Then a career-changing thought.

Move the story into the near future, or as *Mad Max* ambiguously announces in an opening caption: "A few years from now. . ." That nearness in time was a stroke of genius. It allowed the film to portray a society on the downslope to chaos – a pre-apocalyptic moment – making sense of the road wars he planned. And it liberated a comic-book exuberance in the material that would lead all the way to *Fury Road*: Miller could dress his Main Force Patrol up in leathers (how he hated the dull Melbourne police uniform of the seventies) and have them give chase in Kennedy's beloved Ford Falcon XB Sedans painted canary yellow with blue and red stripes like a mohawk. The mania was now logical.

It was also cost-effective. The signature post-apocalyptic future of the four sequels, cradled in an increasingly savage desert, was still way beyond their means. They would find existing locations to embody a decrepit near future. This wasn't simply a convenient backdrop for a roughneck science-fiction B-movie; Miller saw it as prophecy.

In the mid-seventies, the bleak socio-economic picture in Australia was little different from the rest of the world. A global oil crisis had been instigated in 1973, when the OAPEC countries – a cabal of oil-producing Arab nations – embargoed production to protest against American support for Israel during the Yom Kippur War. A dystopia was bleeding out of the evening news: normal folk drawing guns on queue jumpers at Melbourne petrol pumps. A new madness was in the air. How quickly civilisation could crumble, Miller thought.

"People's life-style was threatened, and they were suddenly going after each other," he said. "We had a lot of fun exaggerating that."

Memories lingered of the part Australia played in Vietnam. Young men drifting home with thousand-yard stares. The New World optimism was coming undone.

Whatever the real-world inspiration, Miller and Kennedy were drawing from the films they cherished, as well as the currents in the film industry around them. Their minds had been circling two genres: horror and action. They were heeding the call of commercialism. In their heedless minds, they wanted to revolutionise the car chase, if not action itself. Revive the stunt as a central tenet of cinematic language. Too unruly to fit in with the grace notes of *Picnic at Hanging Rock* or *My Beautiful Career*, *Mad Max* bore the hallmarks of Ozploitation.

Some context. There was the Australian New Wave, which set the critics swooning, and there was Ozploitation, which set Quentin Tarantino swooning. He lends his enthusiasm to the excellent 2007 documentary *Not Quite Hollywood: The Wild, Untold Story of Ozploitation!*. This was his terrain, outrage and provocation, cinema stripped back to its raw, impulsive heart. Following a 1969 arts council report there was a push to make genre films that would never take a bow at Cannes but would satisfy the local market. Beyond period, the New Wave didn't sully itself in genre. Ozploitation wallowed happily in dirt-cheap horror, sci-fi, action, comedy, martial arts, sexploitation and biker flicks like the antipodean cousins of Roger Corman, with their minuscule budgets backed by wealthy investors in search of a tax break. Vulgarity was celebrated. Nudity almost obligatory. They were proudly derivative, with

OPPOSITE: A telling array of wrecks in the scrapyard at Cooma, New South Wales in 1973. *Mad Max* was born out of the reckless car culture of Australia that George Miller had grown up with. Teens would race each other along those long stretches of road. Collisions were a given.

ABOVE: Peter Weir's transcendent period piece *The Picnic at Hanging Rock* embodies everything the Australian New Wave stood for: gossamer images, the contrast between colonial life and landscape, and an experimentation with form.

fading American stars like Stacy Keach and Dennis Hopper moonlighting alongside local actors. Some of them were very good indeed.

A direct connection can be made between *Mad Max* and 1974 Ozploitation biker classic *Stone*. Cult hit to cult hit. *Mad Max*'s near future lies close enough in spirit to the grungy present-day Sydney of *Stone*. Both films feature cops and gangs. Only in Sandy Harbutt's *Stone*, the lone lawman (Ken Shorter) goes undercover among outlaw bikers to flush out a killer (it's *Point Break* long before *Point Break*), and the gang is portrayed with a countercultural noblesse. Nevertheless, Harbutt doesn't stint on brutality. Such prominent *Mad Max*-ers as Roger Ward, Vince Gil, Reg Evans, David Bracks and Hugh Keays-Byrne (as the LSD-loaded Toad) feature in the cast list. There is that same gonzo-Dickensian timbre in the names: Tart, Stinkfinger, Midnight, Septic, Skunk, et al. As frequently pointed out by those dousing for the waters of inspiration, they include a character named "Bad Max."

To prove that all categories have rickety fences, Weir's 1974 debut, *The Cars That Ate Paris*, another huge influence on Miller, tells a riotous, horror-inflected tale of a whole town that ensnares outsiders in car accidents, making off with both mechanical and body parts. Filmed at Watte Flat, New South Wales, it is a mongrel of both New Wave and Ozploitation,

ABOVE: The porcupine Beetle from Peter Weir's *The Cars That Ate Paris*. Weir's first film, a car-crash horror movie comedy, would be a huge influence on *Mad Max*. So much so, this spiky VW would be directly referenced amid the chaos of *Fury Road*.

as well as the Australian subgenre of "car movies" popular in the sixties and seventies of which *Mad Max* would be an exemplar.

Classifications proliferate like mirrors within mirrors. Critic Martyn Conterio describes *Mad Max* as a "misfit movie, a freak among the pack." It's a violent, genre flick, yes, but it has a cinematic power that would translate across the world. Kennedy called it a "highly-sophisticated B-grade film."

Of course, Miller had a theory. He didn't think of *Mad Max* as an exploitation film capturing an audience with the knee-jerk of sensationalism. He went in search of cinema's innate language of show don't tell. "If I make the action sequences as a silent movie," he said, "if it reads as a silent movie, then it can only get better with sound." The ur-text for Max was the mania of Buster Keaton, the stone-faced genius who dreamed up extraordinary visual routines, great capers in which the mechanised world proved endlessly perilous. Keaton would risk life and limb for a laugh. Dangling from trams, leaping between cars, swinging on drainpipes. And something more profound. He created an existential syntax for cinema. They were all stories of survival.

"I was very influenced by a book written by the critic Kevin Brownlow called *The Parade's Gone By*," explained Miller. "He said the main part of the parade has gone by the advent of sound. . . This new language that we called cinema had mostly evolved in the silent era. What differentiated it from theatre were the action pieces, the chase pieces."

Watch *Mad Max 2* or *Fury Road* in all their kinetic mastery and stoic Max is Buster Keaton reborn to dangle again in the winds of fate. This is the visual language of silent cinema. That capacity to join a sequence of images together to form a gag. Set-up to punchline. And it begins in the first film. There is a poetry in *Mad Max*, still rough, but outlandish and thrilling.

What was it about the name? It ran off the tongue so easily. Mad. Max. During post-production, distributers Village Roadshow fretted that it sounded like a comedy. According to a company memo, the film was briefly known as *Heavy Metal*. Though essentially meaningless, it had a certain eye-catching heft. But as they closed in on release, managing director Graham Burke awoke at 3am, certain they should revert to *Mad Max*. Fate was having its say. It was more than a name, more than a character even. It was a statement of intent.

MAX

"FORTUNATELY, NO ONE WAS KILLED."

– GEORGE MILLER

The outskirts of Melbourne gave way to a patchwork of paddocks, flat to the ocean, partitioned by a grid of ramrod-straight highways that begged for speed. The call of the horizon, the needle flicking 100 mph. People forget how green the first *Mad Max* movie is – how this is a story set in a near future, before the apocalypse. There are fields and forests, and the clutter of civilisation: cafes, shops, hospitals and, for what it's worth, a police station. George Miller maintained that the Geelong and Little River suburbs were rundown enough to suggest the screws coming loose on the established order. The place was already a perfect mess. And quiet enough to orchestrate stunts, metal ricocheting across bitumen, without endangering bystanders. Stuntmen were a different matter.

PREVIOUS SPREAD: Death at the wheel – by the final third of *Mad Max*, the hero (Mel Gibson) has been transformed into the spirit of vengeance, with the Interceptor his weapon. The first film is the one truly nihilistic film of the entire saga.

OPPOSITE: The crazy little Australian film that conquered the world – beautifully marketed, *Mad Max*'s fury translated to nearly every country in the world (the big exception: the USA) and held the crown of the most profitable film of all time for many years.

A few years from now, as far as the story is concerned, petrol-drunk criminal gangs are terrorising the highways by bike or supercharged car, while the Melbourne Force Patrol (the "MFP") give chase, a posse of high-speed deputies in canary yellow, most of them halfway mad themselves. Law enforcement amounts to a form of road war, car versus fuel-injected car, kill or be killed. And heading their way is a biker gang bent on a wanton but organised revenge for the death, by car, of one of their number. The Nightrider (Vincent Gil) and his sorry girl Marmaduke (Lulu Pinkus) have come to an explosive end in a stolen Holden HQ Montero in black. Revenge will beget revenge.

Produced by
BYRON KENNEDY

Directed by
GEORGE MILLER

With
MEL GIBSON

Music by
BRIAN MAY

Written by
JAMES McCAUSLAND and GEORGE MILLER

From Warner Bros. A Warner Communications Company.

BELOW: Flying out of the blocks – George Miller threw everything, including arguably all his best stunts, at his opening, ten-minute chase sequence, in which the police Ford Falcons chase the crazed Nightrider in a black Montero.

OPPOSITE: Miller built up the chase sequence silent-movie style through a series of gags, including a Falcon crashing through a despised caravan, filled with cardboard boxes for added effect.

BELOW RIGHT: The sensation of speed was achieved by rigging the camera as close to the surface of the road as possible. In effect, it was the close-ups of the cars that gave the sense of momentum.

Miller and producer Byron Kennedy knew in their bones that their film had to start as others finish, with an extended chase sequence (running to almost ten minutes). In many ways, the best of what they had was going upfront. They shot it last, once they knew what they were doing (relatively). It was a declaration of principles, an overture to Miller's visual music. Something almost physiological. But like everything on their first film, it didn't exactly go to plan.

The chase was already to be underway, with various MFP units in pursuit of their target across the pale flats. "Fuck you" is sprayed on a boulder in Greek in homage to Miller's ancestry. "Do you see me Toecutter? Do you see me?" raves Nightrider, sweating like a pig. As the chase progresses, stunt by crazy stunt, a caravan is shattered, a MFP Pursuit Special rolled, and a Kawasaki sent skidding across the tarmac like a stone. Staging posts in the escalation. Miller throws in almost abstract shots of Max, the hero: close-ups of his sunglasses, glimpses of leather, reflections in a wing mirror. Finally, as Kennedy decreed happily, Nightrider's doomed Montero would be launched skywards via a rocket. Could Kennedy procure anything? As it turned out, Kennedy knew how to get his hands on one. Via the Australian navy.

A Rodinga Booster duly arrives on set from Maribyrnong munitions factory. Along with the rocket comes munitions expert Chris Murray (who will one day blow up the compound in

Mad Max 2), doing the calculations, and predicting a launch speed of 200 mph, at the very least. There are two cameras ready, with Miller stationed behind one and Kennedy the other. They have a getaway car waiting. There is a countdown. The unmanned car launches. But rather than sending the Montero upwards as planned, like a plane taking off, the force of the rocket jerks it free from its cable and straight towards the getaway car containing terrified filmmakers. By a stroke of luck, which would come and go as the *Mad Max* saga sped through the years, it veers off, spinning through 180 degrees and comes to a halt. Everyone keeps their distance until the angry hissing dies down.

Miller declared it another titanic failure. Kennedy was sure they could still use it. And use it they did. A surge of almost absurd momentum, yet shockingly real.

Asked to sum up the making of the first film, Miller would smile serenely and say, well, "Fortunately, no one was killed." He wasn't exaggerating. They were taking chances no film has taken before or since. It was a kind of madness. To create

the stunts they simply did the stunts, or as close as their recklessness would take them. That became set in stone. The audience would never have to suspend disbelief.

Mistakes are the portals to discovery. So said James Joyce, and it was a maxim that Stanley Kubrick, of all directors, would regularly quote. Despite his reputation of being utterly in control, the grand master would improvise entire scenes, willing (and able) to shut down production until he had solved a

BELOW: Joanne Samuel as Max's doomed wife Jessie, clutching their doomed son Sprog (Brendan Heath) – the harrowing scene that fuels the four *Mad Max* films.

ABOVE RIGHT: Max's best friend, Goose (Steve Bisley), a copper who comes a cropper – an unsubstantiated rumour persists that Anthony Edwards's Goose in *Top Gun* was named after Bisley's character.

particular filmmaking riddle. You planned and planned, and then made it up in the moment.

The hot Melbourne hinterlands of October 1977 were about as far across the cinematic universe from *2001: A Space Odyssey* as you could get. But the shooting of *Mad Max* would become living proof of Joyce's theory: out of chaos emerged a legend. A film so much more than the sum of its parts.

Nightrider would prove to be a mere hors d'oeuvre compared to his boss, the aforementioned Toecutter (Hugh Keays-Byrne), who targets the young cop who killed his favourite. An expert driver with a young wife and a kid by the name of Max Rockatansky. Having run from the MFP, and his former life, Max can't escape his fate. Toecutter's gang mow down wife and child in broad daylight (offscreen but symbolised by a child's shoe discarded in the road) and Mad Max is born, bent on revenge.

Miller was still a filmmaker in utero, but he was beginning to express his kinetic theories. How do you capture speed on camera? It was like science, he thought. You needed to capture the texture of the tarmac in relation to the moving vehicle. You need the camera as close to the road as possible, so why not strap it to the bumper, barely inches from the cracked tarmac. "And it had to be widescreen," he said.

Before all this, before Miller began jousting with the fates, a script needed to be

"GEORGE AND I WROTE THE SCRIPT BASED ON THE THESIS THAT PEOPLE WOULD DO ALMOST ANYTHING TO KEEP VEHICLES MOVING."

– JAMES MCCAUSLAND

written. And the director needed help. Miller first met James McCausland in a Sydney boozer. The garrulous New York-born Irish-American journalist had relocated to Australia, where he covered finance for *The Australian*. He was politically astute. He held strong opinions on a range of subjects. Weren't the great Hollywood scribes Ben Hecht and Herman J. Mankiewicz originally journalists? What impressed Miller most was how he would hold forth on the subject of film. They got to know one another, said Miller, "yakking about movies." McCausland could recite entire scenes word-for-word.

Together they developed a theory. How people left the movies recounting all the best moments to each other. Remember when. . . Why not construct an entire film out of those moments? It would take until *Mad Max: Fury Road* to finally realise the dream, but for now Miller handed McCausland his one-page treatment for *Mad Max*.

"Would you like to write a movie?" he asked.

"Why not?" responded McCausland. Not that he had ever written a screenplay or had any idea how.

With the natural rigour of a journalist, he began by researching the present-day fuel crisis, a very real cause for their fragmenting future. As he recalled, "George and I wrote the script based on the thesis that people would do almost anything to keep vehicles moving."

As McCausland made inroads into a screenplay, Miller and Kennedy set about populating their film with both cars and actors.

They had formed Kennedy Miller Productions in 1972. They were fully-fledged partners. To this day – expanded into Kennedy Miller Mitchell Productions with the later addition of producer Doug Mitchell – this is still the company behind the *Mad Max* films. Still with Kennedy's name on the credits. The

"I'VE BEEN GOOFING AROUND ALL MY LIFE. I MIGHT AS WELL GET PAID FOR IT."

– MEL GIBSON

ABOVE: Art imitating life – Mel Gibson and Steve Bisley had been flatmates and bosom buddies at drama school, so it was simple to translate their friendship onto screen.

ABOVE RIGHT: Desperate times call for desperate cops – one of the many advantages of setting the film in the near future was that it allowed Miller to establish an aesthetic by having his cops dress in rock'n'roll leathers rather than dull uniforms.

young producer financed the film to the tune of $350,000 (Australian). All private investors: friends, family, and having knocked on the door of a local stockbroker, a coterie of thirty investors encouraged to throw in a low-risk $10,000 each. It wasn't much, especially for what they had in mind, but they wanted to be free of government assistance and to not ever be, on whatever level, beholden to the film industry.

When it came to casting, said Miller, they didn't want anyone recognisable. Which was a joke, as they couldn't afford anyone recognisable. They would have to discover Max, Goose, Fifi, Jessie, Toecutter and the rest of the gang as a matter of necessity. Necessity, of course, can pay dividends. It would be a film of exuberant performances that stood up to the mayhem. With a fair amount of madness in their method.

Max was elusive. They had met dozens of young men, screen tested some, but it appeared increasingly hopeless. The record shows that the actor James Healey, later to appear in the glossy America soap *Dynasty*, turned them down. Then a casting director suggested they look at a couple of graduates

from the National Institute of Dramatic Arts (known as the "NIDA") in 1977. They were named Mel Gibson and Steve Bisley and shared a pretty ropey house near Bondi Beach. One was blue-eyed, almost ridiculously handsome, if still baby faced. The other had a quick grin and a tougher exterior.

Gibson had a surprising background. For one thing he was American, born in Peekskill, New York, sixth of eleven children, to Hutton and Anna Gibson. His father was a complex man. A World War II veteran, he had worked for the railroad, before falling from a train and damaging his back. While suing the rail company, he won $21,000 on *Jeopardy*. Hutton held to a strict, ultraconservative shade of Catholicism, at one point considering the priesthood. He held a lot of opinions, had even written books on his beliefs, and made sure his views were drummed into his children. When the young Mel was twelve, Hutton took the family to live in Australia, determined that none of his children would be drafted to Vietnam.

Growing up an Australian, his accent swaying to a sonorous, mid-Pacific burr, Gibson was still struck by the reality of American movies in the seventies: *Serpico*, *Dog Day Afternoon*, *The Godfather* films. He saw a future in acting. He certainly had the looks. "I've been goofing around all my life," he announced at his interview for NIDA, "I might as well get paid for it." Months later he was acting in *Waiting for Godot* and alongside

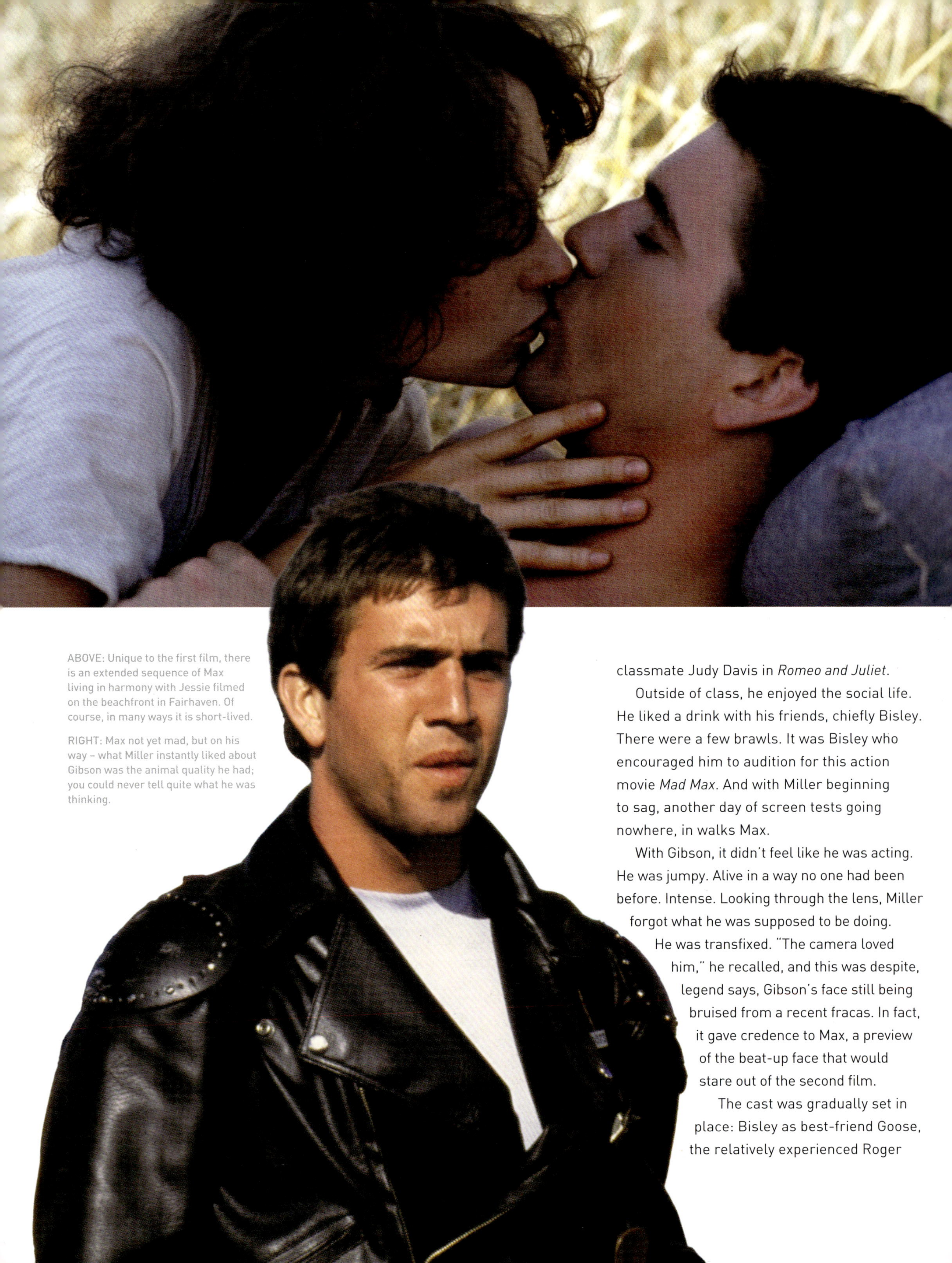

ABOVE: Unique to the first film, there is an extended sequence of Max living in harmony with Jessie filmed on the beachfront in Fairhaven. Of course, in many ways it is short-lived.

RIGHT: Max not yet mad, but on his way – what Miller instantly liked about Gibson was the animal quality he had; you could never tell quite what he was thinking.

classmate Judy Davis in *Romeo and Juliet*.

Outside of class, he enjoyed the social life. He liked a drink with his friends, chiefly Bisley. There were a few brawls. It was Bisley who encouraged him to audition for this action movie *Mad Max*. And with Miller beginning to sag, another day of screen tests going nowhere, in walks Max.

With Gibson, it didn't feel like he was acting. He was jumpy. Alive in a way no one had been before. Intense. Looking through the lens, Miller forgot what he was supposed to be doing. He was transfixed. "The camera loved him," he recalled, and this was despite, legend says, Gibson's face still being bruised from a recent fracas. In fact, it gave credence to Max, a preview of the beat-up face that would stare out of the second film.

The cast was gradually set in place: Bisley as best-friend Goose, the relatively experienced Roger

Ward as police chief Fifi (to save money, Miller crammed his scenes into a single week), and Rosie Bailey as Jessie, Max's young wife. When it came to the gang members, Miller was looking for things to be a little off-key. They are a walking dystopia: Johnny the Boy (Tim Burns), Cundalini (Paul Johnstone), Bubba Zanetti (Geoff Parry), Mudguts (David Bracks). The future's array of alt-Dickensian names is established (a Toecutter could be a biker who cuts corners, rubbing his toes on the tarmac). The film's language was a form of "word salad," said Miller, like sliding the radio between stations. Snatches of local slang, call signs, sobriquets, a pick 'n' mix argot for desperate times. Cops were known as The Bronze.

Keays-Byrne, as the voluminous Toecutter, was an entire concerto in discordant notes. Born in India, of British parentage, his father a colonel, he had been with the Royal Shakespeare Company for six years and knew how to hold a stage. Having emigrated to Australia in 1973 for a change of scene, he had featured in the cult biker hit *Stone* and crime

BELOW: Mob rule – two of the film's sample of collective crazies Johnny the Boy (Tim Burns) and Bubba Zanetti (Geoff Parry). Notice the fabric of Melbourne cityscape in the background.

"WITH GIBSON, IT DIDN'T FEEL LIKE HE WAS ACTING. HE WAS JUMPY. ALIVE IN WAY NO ONE HAD BEEN BEFORE. INTENSE."

saga *The Man from Hong Kong*. He had a way about him, an edge. Burns recalled meeting his co-star for the first time in the foyer of a Sydney theatre. He grabbed him by the face, pulled him close, before bellowing, "Johnny the Boy!" He modelled Toecutter on Genghis Khan.

They couldn't afford to fly the cast anywhere. So Keays-Byrne, already riding the currents that would bring Toecutter to leering life, suggested he and his gang transport their rides from Sydney to Melbourne. Which amounted to running a fleet of brand new

KZ1000s, cajoled out of Kawasaki by the wiles of Kennedy, then future-fitted by French-born motorcycle engineer Bertrand Cadart (who joined the gang as Clunk), across the hard yards of southeast Australia. They could use the three-day trip for some rehearsal – a chance to get into character. Their journey is a legend within the legend.

They conjured up backstories, sleeping in fields, hugging each other against the cold, wearing the same clothes for days, axes and knives stowed on the bikes. Riding into small towns they felt like outcasts, their numbers swelled by real gang members from The Vigilantes Motorcycle Club. The line between fact and fiction became hazy. An honour code was formed to match what was on screen – and an unswerving loyalty to Toecutter.

Somewhere on the backroads of New South Wales the first of the great *Mad Max* tribes was born.

Once in Melbourne, they were prone to pranks of questionable taste, including breaking into Gibson's apartment, trashing the place and pinning a note to the ceiling in red ink (or possibly blood): "We're gonna get you, Bronze." Miller felt the power of these guys, the impact they could have on screen. A twenty-one-year-old Gibson just felt intimidated. Even on set they wouldn't be told what to do. There was genuine tension. Keays-Byrne would never let Toecutter drop, staying permanently in character, beneath a mop of badger-like hair. "It was fantastic," laughed Miller. In hindsight.

"EVEN ON SET THEY WOULDN'T BE TOLD WHAT TO DO. THERE WAS GENUINE TENSION."

For all its limitations, there was a religious devotion to the film from within. They were living *Mad Max*. Such conviction would be contagious in a cinema. Keays-Byrne helped forge the Mad Max ethos.

"He viewed the film as being about people who put up fences and people trying to get around those fences," said Burns.

When he and the boys saw the finished film,

ABOVE LEFT: Hugh Keays-Byrne in *The Man from Hong Kong* (1975) – the British expat actor was relatively established in Australian film but had never delivered quite like this.

OPPOSITE: Toecutter (Hugh Keays-Byrne) on the move – it was the actor's idea that the gang ride their bikes from Sydney to Melbourne before shooting, to get into character. They were supplemented by members of a real biker gang named The Vigilantes.

ABOVE: Toecutter's gang, aka The Zed Runners, aka The Acolytes harked back to the tradition of biker movies like *The Wild Ones*. No one was ever sure how, but producer Byron Kennedy managed to procure a fleet of brand new Kawasakis for the film.

ABOVE RIGHT: The marauding gang – Toecutter leads the charge while clutching a meat cleaver. The actor partly modelled his character on Genghis Khan.

OPPOSITE: Smashing up society – Johnny the Boy takes a pipe to a gleaming motor. In *Mad Max*, law and order is beginning to fragment even before the apocalypse.

they were crestfallen to discover they were the bad guys.

McCausland and Miller completed an impossible 214 pages of script. Every shot was outlined in the utmost detail. Each stunt figured out. On the page, that is. Miller had already made the film in his head. But reality was a different beast. Reality resisted your dreams. Over twelve stinking hot weeks, Miller wrestled with his cast, his script, his crew and the laws of physics.

They never had any permits; it wasn't clear if such things existed. There was nowhere to get a permit from anyway. "It was a legal Twilight Zone," laughed Miller, delighted at his own cheek. Both film and filmmaking were driven by an outlaw spirit. Using police frequencies for their walkie-talkies was certainly illegal. The film subsisted in a loophole; talk of the town. The production had a copy of a letter from the local constabulary granting them freedom to film where they wished, signed by an alleged Sgt. Bloggs. No one has ever tracked down this Officer Bloggs – eyebrows were raised in Kennedy's direction. It became known as their "get out of jail free card."

In any case, the local police came to admire their gusto and ambition. A film had never arrived on their doorstep and they were excited by its depiction of law enforcers on wheels, their cop cars emblazoned in hot red and yellow. After a day's shift dealing with the traffic offences of Melbourne in 1978, they would join the production and bring much-needed help in blocking off roads. Miller recalled their cars being escorted to and from set by a phalanx of police outriders. Which was fairly ironic.

Miller and Kennedy held closed conferences, thick as thieves. At times it was unclear who was the director and who the producer, like the Coen brothers, but without sharing DNA. They were still living together at Kennedy's parents' home in Yarraville. At times, it was as if Kennedy was the only one able to decode Miller's elusive brainwaves. It was as if he was directing freehand. He came

to shoot scenes, action or otherwise (there are those always surprising longueurs with Max and family in their coastal idyl), without storyboards. He would explain what was required.

To establish his heightened ambience, Miller preached anamorphic lenses, which were the stuff of dreams for Australian filmmakers. But Kennedy tracked some down to a Sydney hire shop. A set of genuine Todd-AO anamorphic lenses.

"Wonderfully sharp," said Miller.

"There weren't many to choose from, but enough focal lengths to shoot the movie," remembered cinematographer David Eggby. "They were slow and needed constant recalibration, but they were beautiful bits of glass." It transpired they had previously been used by Sam Peckinpah on *The Getaway* and were pretty scratched up. In the end, only one of them worked. But it was a gift from the moviemaking gods, because it gave them speed.

Eggby was a television veteran, dyed in the wool, certain this young director had little idea what he was talking about. "Can't be done," became an almost daily refrain. There wasn't a day that passed when they didn't butt heads like rams. They were already on the fury road. But for all his truculence, Eggby was bold. He was in the back of the car as Nightrider plays chicken with Max, and he was riding pillion, strapped to Vigilante president Terry Gibson with no more than a leather belt, and no crash helmet, so he could look through the lens at the speedometer as it touched 110 mph. Eggby recalled the speed made the ride smoother and smoother. It was almost a state of grace.

Together with Miller and Kennedy, they devised a miraculous visual style, defeating their lack of budget, skimming the roads and letting the wide angles draw in the landscape.

MFP

"VERY SERGIO LEONE. THE CINEMASCOPE FORMAT WAS PERFECT."

– DAVID EGGBY

PREVIOUS SPREAD: The dark ending of *Mad Max* was highly controversial for its time – the idea that the nominal hero didn't just dispatch the bad guys, but consciously tortured one of them in Johnny the Boy ...

RIGHT: ... who is forced to cuff his ankle to the bumper of car about to explode and left with a hacksaw – either cut off his own foot or go up in flames. Another unsubstantiated rumour persists that this was the inspiration for the *Saw* films.

"Very Sergio Leone," appreciated Eggby. "The Cinemascope format was perfect. This was a different approach to action, it was a once in a lifetime chance to create something that hadn't been done before."

Miller began to work intuitively. He established a fluidity of image and framing. Cause and effect. Connections made between shots. Looking back, by now a director himself, Gibson saw Miller as a genius. He had an ability, he marvelled, "to get the pieces necessary to make a truly compelling in-your-face action sequence." Gibson could never understand what he was doing at the time. But you watched the film and you understood.

To Miller's mind, things were always going wrong. The final scene where Max presents Johnny the Boy with the awful choice of sawing off his foot, handcuffed to the bumper of the car about to explode (*Saw* years before *Saw*), was designed to show how far Max had gone. The light was already failing, and the farmer, on whose land they were shooting, was growing increasingly sceptical about the explosion planned for the end of day. When it came to take two of Max's callous challenge, proof he had now discarded his moral compass, no one could find the keys to the cuffs. It took two hours of searching to find where they had been dropped in the long grass. They got what they needed. But only just.

Even from the very beginning they were dogged by disaster. Stunt co-ordinator Grant Page was supposed to know what he was doing. He was a hardened veteran of Ozploitation shoots. A guy who owned a set of feathers, so he claimed, that had belonged to the legendary Yakima Canutt, stunt double for John Wayne, Errol Flynn and Henry Fonda. He was a stuntie on *Stagecoach*.

ABOVE: The icy-cool Bubba Zanetti armed and dangerous – by the post-apocalyptic *Mad Max 2* guns have been replaced by crossbows, though by *Mad Max: Fury Road* they have been revived with supplies from the Bullet Farmer.

ABOVE RIGHT: Max gets mean with the Grease Rat played by Nick Lathouris, who would return to the franchise as a writer on *Mad Max: Fury Road*.

A week or so into shooting, Miller was pulled over on his way to set with the news that Page had totalled his Kawasaki KZ1000 overtaking Toecutter's convoy at a set of lights and colliding with a semitrailer, with actress Rosie Bailey on the back of his bike. Who hadn't seen who was unclear. What was certain was that both riders had broken their left legs and Page had been struck in the face, leaving his nose smeared across his face. "It's a stunt movie, and the stuntman is gone," remonstrated Miller. And they weren't even filming at the time.

The incident brought everything home to Miller in a sudden rush. He was overwhelmed with panic. The turmoil he almost always kept locked beneath the surface come pouring out like leaking petrol. Everything that could go wrong, all these stuntmen who didn't give a thought to their own safety, a doctor's prognosis of the worst. He was on the phone to Kennedy that afternoon.

"Mate, we can't do this. It's finished. People are going to die."

As Miller would later laugh, philosophically, he had effectively fired himself as director. Kennedy reacted quickly; he had investors on the line. Their inexperience was bleeding into the situation. The producer approached director Brian Trenchard-Smith, who had a reputation for being good with action. He had made *The Man from Hong Kong* with Keays-Byrne. "BTS," as he was known, had a wise head. He refused the offer of *Mad Max* and told Kennedy to shore up the planning. Get the right crew in place. After a late-night heart-to-heart between putative director and producer, best friends, Miller returned to set.

A few days later, Page was back (the unfortunate Bailey had to be replaced with

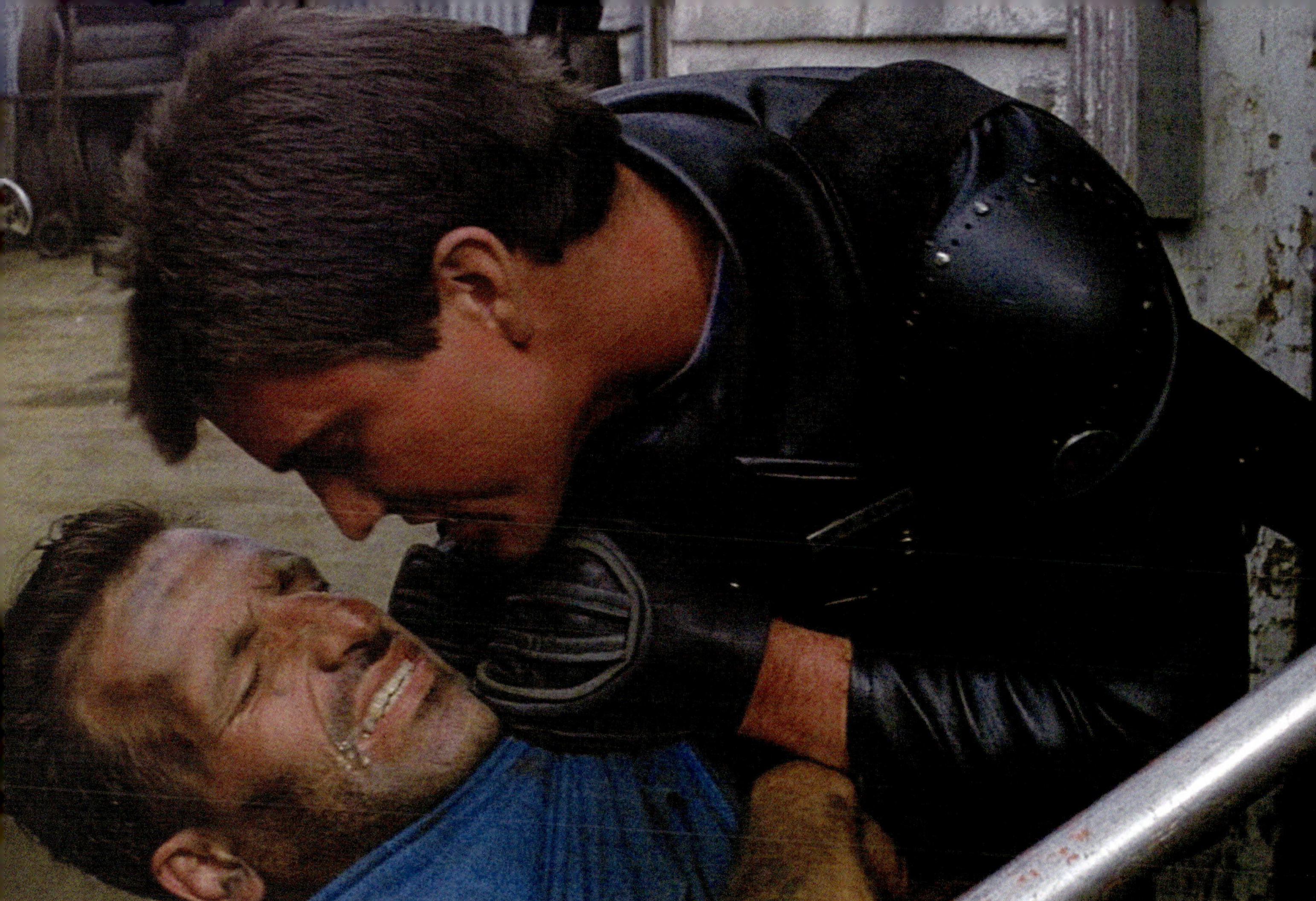

Joanne Samuel), his leg in plaster, face bandaged, black eyes like a panda, co-ordinating stunts from a wheelchair.

"And just to show how unpredictable and monumentally ironic filmmaking is," said Miller, "we then shot for another eleven weeks with a lot of stunts, great speeds, relatively high danger, and there wasn't one injury to anybody."

Not that they didn't come close. The legend of the making of any *Mad Max* film is emblazoned in its daredevil stunts. But with the first film, their methods seem almost quaint by comparison with what was to come, the level of risk recalling those early days of silent cinema that Miller longed to replicate.

Take for instance, the leap from Kirks Bridge Road in Little River. As per Miller's instructions, the set-up had Max, in the Interceptor, scattering a quartet of bikers like skittles, two of whom go flying into the air and land in the river, while two are hurled onto the road. Onlookers in the crew thought Dale Bensch (a Vigilante turned stuntie) had to be dead. He slammed into the railings, and was then rammed by his own bike, before a second bike flipped up and hit him on the back of the head. To everyone's amazement, and steadying Miller's palpitating heart, he got up and dusted himself down. Once he had his neck cracked into place he was ready to go again. Kennedy would watch the footage over and over again.

Page was fit enough to leap from a bike into the river. It was about adrenaline, he said, "it closes down the unnecessary parts of the body and accelerates the brain, the heart, the muscles, giving all the blood to those areas."

And it was about madness.

After a day's filming, the tarmac scattered with debris, Miller and Kennedy would stay behind to sweep the roads. A director and producer armed with brooms.

Whatever satisfaction Miller could take from having survived production was wiped out in the edit room. And by edit room, well, the kitchen of his friend Peter Kamen's house, curls of celluloid spilling onto the parquet floor, the smell of coffee and fried food, serenaded by the nervous hum of an old fridge. After six weeks of using a professional editor, Tony Patterson, another TV veteran unwilling to budge from the tried and tested, they ran out of money. What they had, Miller knew, was a pale version of his film. Necessity was the deciding factor. They

ABOVE: The end of the film, the start of the road – Max leaves Johnny the Boy to his explosive fate and heads off into the future. The greenery of the Melbourne suburbs will be replaced by the blasted terrain of the desert.

would figure it out for themselves. The editing deck was care of the ingenuity of Kennedy's father, who built it from scratch. Kennedy himself was cutting sound in the bedroom, regularly coming into the kitchen to offer comment on the assembly. This ground on for seven months, with Miller going through the film frame-by-frame.

The despair came down upon him again. He was always at war with an internal voice, a ghost critic with his own face. The problem was that compared to his dream film, the footage spooling through his homemade Moviola was a disaster. "*Mad Max*," he would come to say, "had defeated him." The continuity didn't match; the light was inconsistent from one shot to the next; essential pieces of the puzzle were missing, the action clumsy. It was all so laughably amateur. The biggest stuff was "in my head," he despaired. But now it was too late, he had made a terrible film, a jalopy of scenes as mismatched as the warped Maxian contraptions in inconceivable sequels to come. It was just as he had predicted. He

had let everyone down. What right did he have to call himself a director? "I honestly thought I wasn't cut out to make movies," he recalled.

Naively, Miller had thought that if you prepare enough ahead of time, it was only a matter of executing your plans. The lesson was stark and painful: filmmaking was as much about adapting to the forces that are arrayed against you. Swaying with the wind. You found your film in the collision of life and art. In the edit you saved it. Nothing ever went completely to plan. *Mad Max* had hardly gone to plan at all.

Once again, Miller implored Kennedy to be rid of him – to bring in a professional and assemble what they could from the footage. But he had to keep going. Find ways to cheat, to use the cuts to create the *impression* of something. Film was at its deepest level an illusion of movement. If you cut skilfully enough, fast enough, the brain would assemble the stunt for you.

It was unlikely he considered himself in such grand terms, sitting in a messy Melbourne kitchen day after day, but he was progressing editing principles set down by the Soviets, and pursued by D. W. Griffith: the power of cross-cutting, parallel images, montages, the construction of meaning through time.

For the death of wackadoodle Toecutter, unconventionally the second-to-last to fall in Max's icy-calm killing spree, Miller

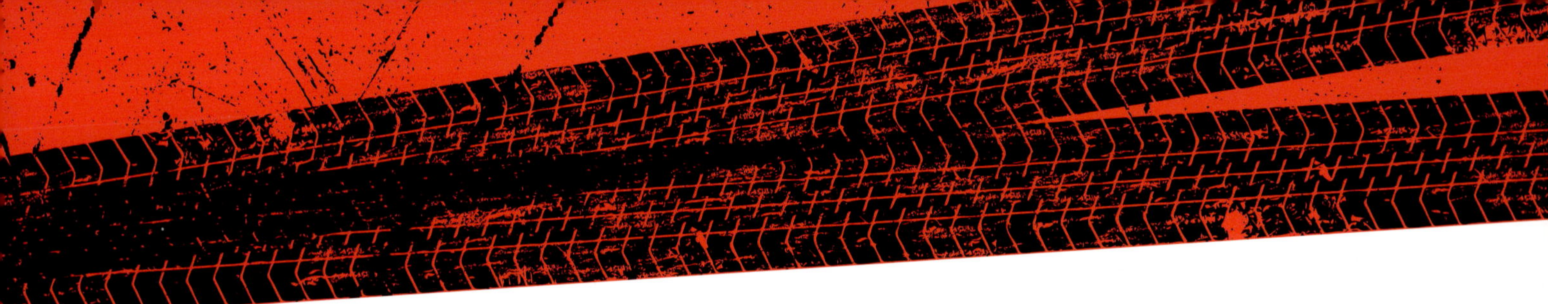

planned a collision between bike and oncoming truck. It was an action motif that would be repeated in every *Mad Max* film to come. Head-on smashes – like kids with toys. Cars or bikes reduced to splintering metal. Miller didn't know it yet, but he was accumulating a language with which he would continually reinvent the tenets of the chase sequence. A familiar fragrance, as rich as petrol fumes, would tie the films together. And no matter how big his budgets, the editing process would send him into paroxysms of despair from which he would have to imagine his way out.

In the quicksand of the edit, Miller discovered an aesthetic for his raw sci-fi. Dialogue was for wimps. "My rule in editing action is that you should cut it like a silent movie, so that if you watch it without sound you'll miss very little." The Buster Keaton method: let the images tell the story. "I mean, some of the cuts are fast because of sheer embarrassment about the shoot," he admitted.

Which included the end of Toecutter. The Kenworth twelve-wheeler was borrowed, and the truck driver had, understandably, protested that smashing a bike into the front grille was going to cause a fair amount of damage. Draw back and take in the whole of the sequence and it sings with Miller's growing assurance. *Mad Max* is evolving into *Mad Max 2*: the dance between hurtling asphalt, hub-level sweeps of bike and Interceptor – right to left, left to right – rear views of the oncoming car. Peering in through the windscreen at a dead-eyed Max. Those perspective shots of the rising topography – moving along the z-axis, into the screen – with the oncoming traffic out of sight. It was like a short story building to a twist, a cataclysmic punchline. But to protect the front of the truck, the art department had hastily attached a false plate to the grille, and it looked as if an eight-year-old had painted it. It was so obviously fake it was a joke.

Without any hope of reshoots, Miller manufactured a distraction. So much of the *Mad Max* effect was simply triage. A stroke of genius was improvised in the lounge. The momentary insert of Toecutter's protruding, bloodshot, latex eyes, squeezed through a mocked-up face by hand. A vision of a vision of

BELOW: It's all in the eyes – in an inspired move, during post-production George Miller filmed a few frames of Toecutter's protruding latex eyeballs to land the shock of his death under an encroaching truck.

OPPOSITE: But eyes are a running motif in all the films – it goes back to the methods of silent film again, without words, it is the eyes that convey meaning.

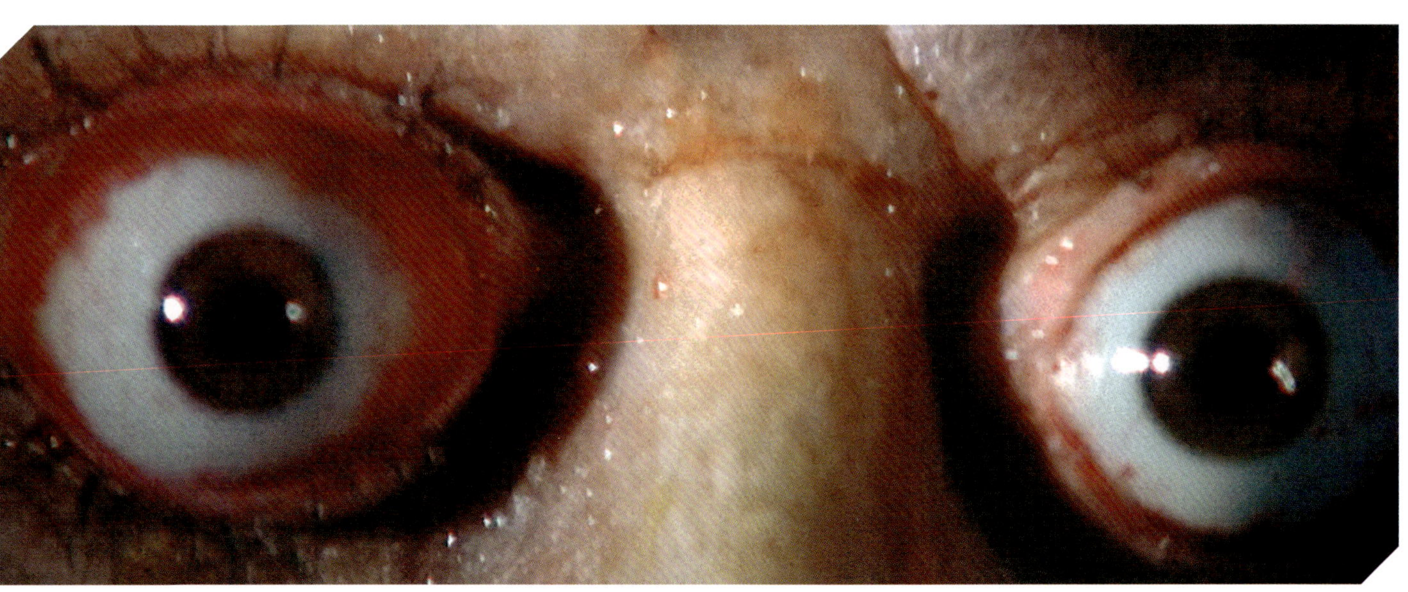

incoming death. Hitchcock on wheels. Eye-popping cinema! And another motif to be added to the mix of future collisions. Wez's demented eyeballing in *Mad Max 2*. The Bullet Farmer's blinded eyes in *Fury Road*.

Miller recalled meeting those New Wavers Philip Noyce and Peter Weir at a festival, to his mind talents far beyond his meagre resources. He told them *Mad Max* was a mess of his own making; nothing had gone to plan. "George, all movies are like that," responded Weir. "You're like a patrol in the jungle: you don't know where the snipers are, but you have to finish the job." Miller finessed his own metaphor. Making films, he mused, "was like walking a really big dog." You want to go one way, but the dog has other ideas.

Miller claimed *Mad Max* is only twenty-five per cent of what he imagined.

It remains a mystery to him why *Mad Max* worked. He considered the finished film unreleasable. "That film is almost like a deformed child to me," he recalled in that odd combination he has of wry and woebegone. To this day he can't shake what he sees as its failings, though he at least looks upon his career-making firstborn a little more fondly. Like Kennedy, there were plenty of others who could see what he was blind to. The power of *Mad Max*. That mix of visceral forward motion, storytelling and bitter wit. Coming out of a rough cut towards the end of 1978, Graham Burke, Village Roadshow's seen-it-all managing director knew he had never seen anything like this before. Forgetting the car he had parked nearby, he walked home buzzing, eager to spread the word. He began calling friends and colleagues: "I've just seen the greatest Australian film."

ABOVE: George Miller was disconsolate with the results of his first film, blind to the power of his imagery and the outrageous sense of humour that fuelled them. *Mad Max* became a sensation.

OPPOSITE: Birth of an icon – the image of Mel Gibson's Max was fully established in the first film with the leg braced with a spanner, the leathers, and the shotgun. He would be as indelible as the Man With No Name.

While so many critics cheered (and cheer still) – "Clearly the work of a natural filmmaker," enthused *The Guardian* – there would be an equal and opposite backlash in certain quarters of the local media. An undercurrent of controversy foretelling of copycat violence and likening the film's effect to that of Kubrick's *A Clockwork Orange*. The deputy president of the Australian Crime Prevention Council announced that "even though it was made in Australia, it should be banned in Australia." It was banned for years in New Zealand and landed an X certificate in liberal France. Social commentator and self-described humanist Phillip Adams saw a film filled with "incipient Mansons."

Which all seems so preposterous now. *Mad Max* is the most influential Australian film ever made, and the most profitable. The greatest? Maybe not. But Miller was wrong. Rough-edged but riotous, he had made quite a film, a thunderclap over the tidy lawns of the Australian New Wave.

The premiere was on 12 May 1979 at Melbourne's East End cinema, long gone with the arrival of multiplexes that would carry *Mad Max Beyond Thunderdome* and *Mad Max: Fury Road*. To Miller's amazement, the audience was soon whooping, caught up in the surge, in Toecutter's deranged antics, screaming as Max tears his Interceptor along unbending roads, monomaniacal with revenge.

"*Mad Max* wasn't slick and it didn't look very elegant, but it grossed more than $100 million world-wide," mused Miller, from the vantage point of unforeseen success. "The only market it didn't perform well in was the United States, where it went out in a disastrously dubbed print that had all the warriors speaking like dropouts from a mail-order acting school."

While Warner Brothers would release the film globally, American International Pictures (an exploitation outfit looking for a quick buck) handled it in the States, and decided the Australian accents and slang terminology would be indecipherable at a Poughkeepsie drive-in. The result was laughable. America would have to wait for *The Road Warrior*.

In the meantime, Miller and Kennedy paid back their investors, the profit margins beyond their wildest expectations. They then bought a cinema. The Metro Theatre in Kings Cross, Sydney, was their new base of operations. They then wondered what the future might hold.

WARRIOR

"THERE HAS BEEN TOO MUCH VIOLENCE, TOO MUCH PAIN."

– LORD HUMUNGUS

The silver mines had made Broken Hill a boomtown. Which was a relative distinction. The bustling outpost lay in the far west of New South Wales, the heart of the outback, over eight hundred miles from Sydney, surrounded by an ocean of sand and scrub, a language of wind-stunted shrubs stretching pancake-flat into the distance beneath the vast pale-blue shell of sky. Seventy per cent of this continent was desert. To get a whole crew out to the middle of nowhere, reflected George Miller, "was one of our more significant achievements."

By day it was an oven, by night an ice box. But the roads were just right, undulating over the plain, and the speed limit was whatever you wanted.

As preordained by the Miller method, *Mad Max 2* begins in motion. It will be ever thus, across five films, as if there is no pause for breath between stories, even if there were years and then decades between productions. Max one gear shift ahead of his pursuers. At bumper lever, the Interceptor eats up highway. On its tail comes a Kawasaki Z1 900 motorbike, a black Ford Landau with a skull for a hood ornament, and a VW dune buggy done up like *The Flintstones*. Their occupants are clothed in varying intensities of leather, one of them crowned with a red mohawk. In production terms, they were ten miles north of Broken Hill, cresting a low rise, then swooping down onto the Mundi-Mundi plain. The soil was as red as Mars. Gone is the impressionistic assault of *Mad Max*. The world is

PREVIOUS SPREAD: Old Blue Eyes – Mel Gibson as Max at the wheel of his Interceptor. What George Miller loved about his leading man was the aura of a wild animal, beautiful but unreachable.

OPPOSITE: The quintessential shot of Max, descending the rise at Red Hill with sawn-off shotgun, rocking leathers, leg brace, and faithful companion.

more violent and raw, but the choreography is assured. The pieces slot together like a dance. Max slaloming between the debris of recent roadkill and a plume of oily smoke. The sensation of speed is absolute. Until that endlessly copied gag of Max jamming on the brakes, freezing forward momentum, just as the Landau driver fires a bolt, piercing the biker's arm instead. The crossbows were Byron Kennedy's idea.

Seeing off his foes, Max returns to scavenge the precious "guzzaline" leaking from the wreck. A body tumbles from the cab, eyes bulging out of a glass-flayed face in homage to Ben Gardner's bloated corpse in *Jaws*, surely, and Toecutter's fate in *Mad Max*. That rig will prove pivotal. Dystopian Chekov. Down its flank in graffitied yellow letters: "The vermin have inherited the Earth."

The biggest shift in *Mad Max 2*, said Miller, was in his head. "By the time we got to the second *Mad Max* movie, we went with the flow. That's the difference between the two films – on one I was prepared to be bewildered, on the other I was shocked by my bewilderment." Always so humble, rooted in Aussie soil. The potential of the first *Mad Max* was unleashed in

ABOVE LEFT: Max scours the Compound with a telescope. The post-apocalyptic future of *Mad Max 2* was imagined almost in terms of stepping back in time.

ABOVE RIGHT: Max scavenges sacred "guzzaline" from a wreck. Gibson had returned enthusiastically to his signature role with the sure knowledge that he already had Hollywood deals set up.

the second. This is the work of a virtuoso. The first of Miller's masterpieces. One of the most influential of all films, certainly in action terms. Guillermo del Toro, a disciple like so many, came out of the theatre and heedlessly lay down on the road so he could study the grain of the asphalt. "The way I looked at the world couldn't be the same," he said.

In 1981, Kennedy was bewildered by its

reception. "I understand that Steve Spielberg saw *The Road Warrior* and admired it. I don't know exactly what that means because that's about seventeenth hand, but I'm sure that he and George Lucas can see the same kind of rapport with which they approach the business of filmmaking."

Full circle. Where once Miller and Kennedy had been inspired by American movies, generations of filmmakers, names such as del Toro, Quentin Tarantino, Robert Rodriguez, Edgar Wright, the Hughes and Coen brothers, and Zack Snyder, have sought to

"THE VERMIN HAVE INHERITED THE EARTH."

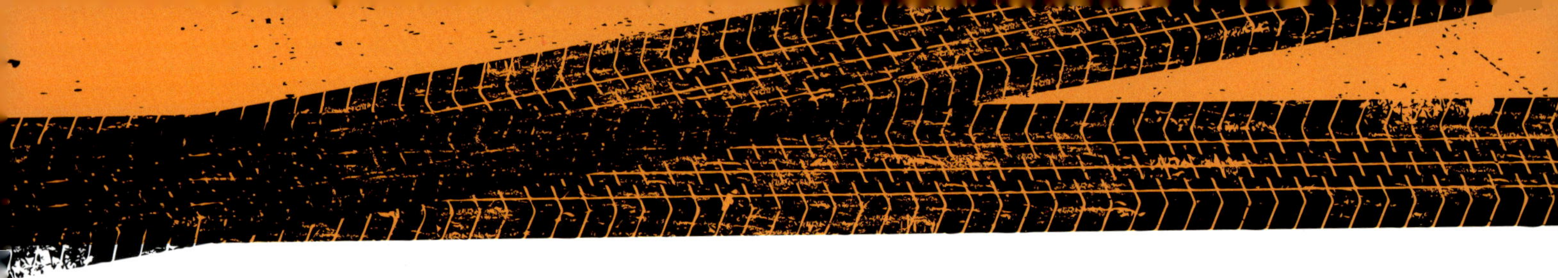

capture its visceral energy. It is one of the films that enflamed James Cameron into becoming a director – *The Terminator* would plunder its metallic fury and aesthetic sheen.

This was "a film of pure action, of kinetic energy organized around the barest possible bones of a plot," wrote Roger Ebert, directing the cinemagoing traffic from his column in the *Chicago Sun-Times*. You could jot the story down on a postcard (from the edge), sum it up to a friend over a beer, but Max's world resonated with a growing mythology as sand-blown and vast as John Ford. This was science fiction but closer in tone to the westerns not only of Ford, but Sergio Leone's Spaghetti trilogy. Only in this desert the man has a name.

As Miller put it, in that plain, deprecating manner: "*The Road Warrior* was really an act of atonement for *Mad Max*." Known simply as *Mad Max 2* around the world and *The Road Warrior* within America, where the *Mad Max* brand still had no currency, the sequel was a chance to make peace with the first film. The calls for a second had been almost immediate: Max had driven off into the rain, alive if not sane. He was out there somewhere. And with the money rolling in, why not? Wasn't this how Hollywood worked? Still rattled by his experience making his debut, Miller resisted. Nevertheless, he and Kennedy found themselves trying to fathom what had made their film so exciting to audiences, despite everything. How had it resonated in France as much as Sweden as much as Japan, everywhere in fact apart from America?

"At first we went for the obvious," said Miller. "It's a violent, exciting film." Yet plenty of films fit those criteria and they hadn't

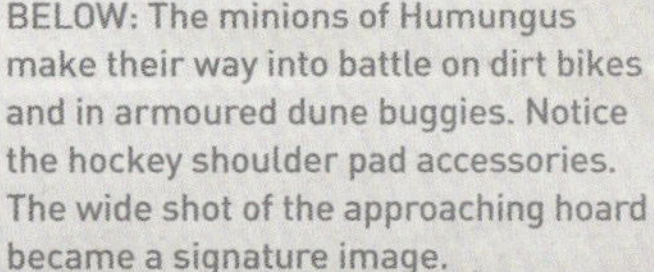

BELOW: The minions of Humungus make their way into battle on dirt bikes and in armoured dune buggies. Notice the hockey shoulder pad accessories. The wide shot of the approaching hoard became a signature image.

become the most profitable of all time. Perusing erudite, European critics, he began to understand something about *Mad Max*, which had occurred purely by instinct. Out there on the roads north of Geelong they had tapped into a remote branch of the Jungian collective consciousness, the monomyth that held all stories together. What you might call a public dream. In Scandinavia, Max was perceived as a Viking. In France, already attuned to American genres, they saw him in western terms, the drifting gunslinger. In Japan, he was a Samurai. Miller had never seen Kurosawa before, but after watching *Yojimbo* he knew that, in his own crude way, Max was a kindred spirit to Toshiro Mifune's lone ronin.

"That's when we got into Joseph Campbell."

The start of a lifelong obsession, he became convinced that *Mad Max* was rooted in a tradition that connected Homer to King Arthur to Aboriginal Dreamtime. The New York mythologist Campbell had worked with Jung, studied religion, pondered dreams, deciphered Joyce and inspired *Star Wars*. His seminal work, *The Hero with a Thousand Faces*, proposed that hero myths from every culture could be distilled into one hero myth, an archetypal figure – a solitary, amoral character who wanders a dark wasteland. Miller was electrified by the idea. Medicine had taught him that nature operates according to the laws of physics and chemistry, entropy and motion, blood and petrol. Campbell presented him with the idea that the nature of humankind is conjoined by storytelling, a force that reaches back thousands of years into the past and into the mists of the future. All stories, in the end, the former doctor concluded, were a way of "confronting death."

ABOVE: Max makes his bid for neutrality as he slips away from the Compound with his tally of precious "guzzaline" – a great benefit of The Pinnacles in New South Wales were the views offered onto the plain below. Everything in the sequel got so much bigger.

ABOVE RIGHT: Ready for what was in store on the second film, Miller works his magic with a weary-looking cinematographer Dean Semler (left) and Gibson awaiting instructions (right).

"Ladies and gentlemen, boys and girls," Dr. Dealgood announces in *Mad Max Beyond Thunderdome*, "dyin' time's here."

Miller began to think of himself not as a director but a storyteller. Homer of the barren highways. The critic David Chute, plying his thoughts in *Film Comment*, saw the truth: "The *Max* movies are hallucinatory fairy tales masquerading as crash-and-burn genre films."

Their pulses quickening, Miller and Kennedy began to speculate about what the first movie could have been. What a *Mad Max* movie might yet be. They set aside a rock 'n' roll themed *Cyrano de Bergerac* called *Roxanne* (which bears no relation to the Steve Martin version of 1986), and began work on a sequel that, for Miller, would resolve every mistake he had made. In doing so, he would refine his original concept into base cinematic and mythological impulses. Pure storytelling.

This was no cynical cash-in. It was hardly the same world. The same character, the same car, maybe, but *Mad Max* had been "an outer-suburban biker movie," said Kennedy. This thing, he concluded with relish, "is so obviously a fantasy and on another planet that you could never call it a sequel." They were nuking the paradigm.

Much like James McCausland before him, Terry Hayes had no idea how to write a screenplay. English-born, he was another fished out of the pool of journalism, working for the *Sydney Morning Herald*. Stationed in New York as foreign correspondent, still only twenty-one, he had covered Watergate. He brought a similar worldliness to McCausland.

Australia may have a large land mass, laughed Hayes, but it had a small population. "This guy, who was a former doctor, arranged to meet me through a mutual acquaintance," he recalled.

"I've directed this movie," Miller told him, "it's terrible."

A font of anecdotes and shrewd interpretation, Hayes is a significant contributor to the history of *Mad Max*. Having first hired him to write the novelisation of *Mad Max*, once its success warranted such a thing, Miller was impressed enough to make another proposal. Did he want to help him write a screenplay for a sequel? Hayes threw himself into the same theories of storytelling, devouring Campbell. He realised that identical impulses governed journalism, novels and screenplays: "You must, whatever it is, make it believable."

Then it was a case of stripping it down to its bones. "Screenplays are Darwinian," Miller informed him, "it's the fight to survive, it's only the survival of the fittest as far as ideas, words, dialogue, everything."

Running on a nervous, jittery energy not unlike The Gyro Captain, Hayes cut an unlikely figure out in the desert, but the success of *Mad Max 2* would make him one of the leading screenwriters in Australia: *Mad Max Beyond Thunderdome*, *Bodyline*, *Dead Calm*, *Bangkok Hilton*, Mel Gibson's *Payback*, *Vertical Limit*. But it is always *Mad Max 2* that leads his introductions. It is always *Mad Max 2* that reporters want to talk about. "It was like Orson Welles," he joked, "I started at the top and worked my way down."

Intent on tapping into the Jungian well, Miller spent much of the writing period lying on the floor half asleep. "I was putting my unconscious mind at work," he insisted. They were staying on the Mornington Peninsula of Western Port Bay in Victoria, and when Miller was upright, they took walks through the beaches and mud flats, dune scrub and grasslands, discussing what shape the new story would take. Sensibly, an early idea of setting their *Mad Max* story on the oceanfront was abandoned (when water was eventually applied to the *Max* aesthetic the result was *Waterworld*), but the view of a petrochemical works began another career-defining chain reaction.

Go further into the future.

With the help of a third musketeer in Brian Hannant (who also served as first assistant director), the sequel is set after the apocalypse brewing in the first: a montage of newsreel footage (images from World War II and other episodes of human iniquity) recalls "the blaze that engulfed them all." The footage gives way to a recap of *Mad Max*. "Only those mobile enough to scavenge, brutal enough to pillage would survive," the grave narrator

continues. There is a new shot of Max in his old uniform by the graveside of his wife and son, veiled in smoke like a fading memory. Max, we are told, is "a man who wandered out into the Wasteland." The old shot of the Interceptor driving through the rain gives way to a road cutting through the hardscrabble desert and the gasp of a supercharger.

Barely eighteen months had passed since the original film, but Gibson's Max looks as if he has aged a decade, but the camera still can't resist him. Between films, Gibson's face had leaned down to the classical bone structure of a Hollywood leading man, only his hair is tousled in grey at the temples, his square jaw unshaven, his blue eyes unreadable, and his left leg slung in a brace from the bullet wound in the first film. The picture is clear – Max has gone feral. His only companion is a raggedy mutt.

Over one hundred dogs had failed the

audition, when animal handler Dale Aspin drove Miller to the RSPCA pound in Yagoona, Sydney. As soon as they walked in, this ugly-looking blue heeler dropped a rock at Miller's feet. Miller was smitten and Aspin reassured he could be trained. It turned out he was due to be euthanised the next day. For Miller, this salt-and-pepper mutt was, like the car, an extension of Max. The unnamed dog has a red scarf around its neck; Max has one around his arm. They have the same haircut. Max gobbles up a can of Dinki-Di dog food, sharing the remnants with his companion. Dinki-di is slang for steadfast.

In an early draft of the screenplay, the dog had three legs to match the lame antihero. There is a tale of Miller, blindly compelled by his story, wondering aloud about the possibility of amputating the leg off a dog only to be silenced by the appalled reaction of his team. Even Kennedy was shocked. Their four-legged debutant proved a trooper, once acclimatised to the low growl of the engines. Early on, having relieved himself in the Interceptor, an enterprising crew member plugged his ears with cotton wool. At the end of production, he was adopted by one of the stuntmen.

"A GIRL GETS IT, A DOG GETS IT, EVERYBODY GETS IT."

– MEL GIBSON

Gibson would be adopted by another country. His stardom was gathering its own momentum: *Mad Max* had led to Peter Weir's New Wave smash *Gallipoli* (which had doubled

ABOVE LEFT: George Miller was gratified at how, in barely eighteen months, Mel Gibson seemed to have aged years from the smooth-faced Max of the original. It spoke to the burden he carried.

LEFT: Negotiations *Mad Max*-style – Max gets the better of the duplicitous Gyro Captain (Bruce Spence). The entire film is a study in personal survival, but an alliance, even a bond, of sorts is formed between the warrior and pilot.

ABOVE: Max and his spirit animal, the unnamed mutt, discovered in a Sydney pound. Miller wanted the animal to be an extension of the man. They even resembled one another.

their Australian box office). Hollywood was growing curious. Deals were in the offing. The window of affordability was closing. His magnetic presence still cost them an estimated $120,000 compared to $15,000 on the original. In any case, he was encouraged by what the new film offered. Max was different. He was indifferent. Bent on survival. Adapting to circumstance, he is now distinctly an Eastwood-like figure, rugged against the pale landscape. Gibson appreciated the script's nihilism. "It didn't spare anyone: people flying under the wheels, a girl gets it, a dog gets it, everybody gets it."

Like Max, the entire world has gone to hell. They went in search of a defining desert, arid and rocky, but still imprinted with roads. The brush stroke of the old order. A budget of $4 million, then the most expensive Australian production (how quickly their world had changed), allowed them to scout the desert by helicopter, in search of emptiness. The Woomera Range in South Australia had a fitting resonance given it was once a nuclear test site, but the military authorities led them a dance until finally pulling out. Miller proposed the salt flat of Island Lagoon, until Kennedy pointed out that if they had any rain, which they did, the set would sink.

It was one of the first films to shoot in Broken Hill, but the mining town offered a lot of infrastructure. "I mean there was a French restaurant for god's sakes," marvelled Miller. "And you had all that technology that they use in mines for welding and all the artisans." Beyond the edge of town, in the shadow of three humpbacked mountains somehow known as The Pinnacles, there was the perfect expanse on which to build their compound.

In Miller's forwards-backwards aesthetic this heavily guarded petrol refinery is like a medieval castle besieged by marauders and the most expensive set ever built in Australia. And the largest. *Mad Max* was transcending the gestalt categories of New Wave or Ozploitation to become a national industry in its own right. The encampment was the centre of the production and the

ABOVE LEFT: Leader of the progressive Compound, Pappagallo (Mike Preston) attempts to enrol Max into his plans for escape. The name Pappagallo referred to his long-lost job as an oil executive, roughly translating to "father of the gallon."

ABOVE: The Captain's Girl (Arkie Whitely) samples the questionable charms of The Gyro Captain. The Kiwi actor Spence played The Gyro Caption as an inversion of Max: jabbering, uncool but still in touch with his humanity.

heart of the story.

The plot was simple. Pure, Miller would say. Before production, he had his actors and department heads watch two key films. Alan Ladd riding in from the wilderness to save the ranchers in *Shane*. Mifune's warrior playing all sides against the middle in *Yojimbo*. Miller's story falls between the two. Max is caught in the middle of the conflict between Lord Humungus's open-road barbarians and Pappagallo's petrol-farming progressives behind their tyre walls. Each collective has re-established a social structure, with hierarchies and hopes. Max is the only solo act. Apart from another stray, a most peculiar fellow named in the script as The Gyro Captain (Bruce Spence), for he has at his disposal, in another Kennedy whim, a gyrocopter. Pappagallo (Mike Preston) and his pale-clad crew dream of the coast, two thousand miles away, and a new beginning, but they need to break free of the siege with a precious cargo of fuel. Recalling the rig from the start of the film, Max concludes that he is the getaway driver they need. "You want to get out of here? You talk to me," he sneers. It's virtually a monologue for Max. The third act is in effect a single, unfettered chase sequence.

The subversive, horror movie delinquency of the first film is stripped away to be replaced with, as Chuck Bowen waxed lyrical in *Slant*: "a poetic action sonata of cars and leather that's rich in beautifully composed wide shots." True enough, but the power of *Mad Max 2* lies in Miller portraying his blasted future in human terms. To an extent, Max's trajectory is no longer light to dark, sane to mad. He is rediscovering his humanity, or a sliver of it. Max is doing a twisted version of the right thing. It's a transaction – for fuel – but there begins a thematic reintegration that will serve as the emotional current of both *Thunderdome* and *Fury Road*.

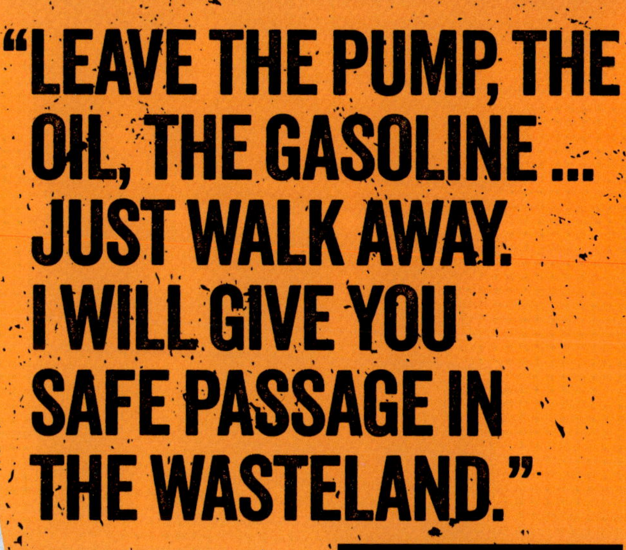

With the help of Hayes and Hannant, and contributions from the actors, Miller constructed backstories for his characters. Max already had a history in the events of the first film, but Lord Humungus, for instance, with his bodybuilder's frame and Cooper HM6 hockey mask insinuating a hideously scarred face beneath (he clearly has no ears), was a former military officer ravaged by an explosion. "He was a fairly mature individual, a kind of strategist," expanded Miller, "not just a crazed hot-head. . ." Inside the box in which he keeps his prized Smith & Wesson revolver are glimpsed old medals and photos, Kurtz-like artefacts of a former existence.

Beneath the mask, Kjell Nilsson almost quit on his first day it was so cold. Temperatures Broken Hill hadn't seen for 120 years. A hoarfrost greeted him outside the hotel. The former Olympic weightlifter was no stranger to ice, having grown up in Gothenburg, Sweden, before coming to Sydney to train the Swedish weightlifting team for the Moscow Olympics and part-time work as a nightclub bouncer. Miller knew he had his "Ayatollah of Rock and Rolla" within minutes of meeting him. Six foot four, 250 lbs, ripped: Nilsson was exactly what the director had in mind.

All the same, stepping into the wind in barely more than a codpiece and cervical collar was a shock to the system. He would swear under his breath – a mantra: "bullshit, bullshit, bullshit" – determined to get every scene in a single take.

Co-star Vernon Wells couldn't believe his eyes. "Have you done any blue movies?" he gawped.

Nilsson took exception to that.

They were already channelling the power dynamics of the gang. Commander and attack dog. Without the all-consuming presence of Hugh Keays-Byrne's Toecutter, Miller effectively split his arch-villain into three characters for the sequel: Humungus is the body (and brains); Max Phipps as The Toadie, with the Davy Crocket hat and incongruous specs, is the mouthpiece; and Wells, as mohawk crested Wez, is the deranged lieutenant and Max's dark reflection.

OPPOSITE: The mighty, masked Lord Humungus (as played by former Swedish Olympian weightlifter Kjell Nilsson) makes his authoritarian speeches via an old-time PA system. Each of the *Mad Max* films will offer up a darkly funny demagogue, a reminder of how mankind got into this mess.

Wells grew up in the Australian sticks. Rushworth, Victoria was another Chinchilla with only a single shop and a single school with a single teacher. Escaping to Melbourne, he fronted bands, made a name for himself, and got taken on by an agency, then local television shows. Miller's girlfriend, Sandy Gore, had seen him on stage in the nudity-prone *Hosanna* (Gibson was also in the audience). He was fearless, she told Miller. A month later he was doing a costume test for the sequel. Brought before the director, Wells caught his reflection in a mirror for the first time and the sight of his butt hanging out of leather chaps.

"Holy fuck!" he exclaimed.

BELOW: Vernon Wells as the iconic nutball Wez, Humungus's mohawk-crowned attack dog in bottomless chaps. The future fashion came care of Norma Moriceau, one of the foremost designers in London's punk scene.

ABOVE: The Humungus takes aim at The Gyro Captain (or at least the stunt Bruce Spence). Aside from Max's shotgun, the despot's treasured revolver is the only gun seen in the entire film.

"That's it," the director grinned to costume designer Norma Moriceau.

Wells worked with Miller on a backstory for wild Wez. He was another vet, trained to know weapons, gifted with vehicles. Miller instructed him to imagine life after an apocalypse. Now imagine a supermarket stacked with canned goods and bottled water. Enough for twelve months. What do you do? Take the place, replied Wells. What if your neighbours came to take it from you, asked Miller? He would defend it, of course.

"Welcome to the film," said Miller.

"You could be a lawyer, a doctor or a garbage man," said Wells. "It didn't matter. The will to survive is stronger than all that shit."

Humungus's gang was far more intently imagined than Toecutter's mob. This was comic-book fetishising long before the genre had a stranglehold on cinema. Bad guys demarcated by their outrageous plumage. A *Mad Max* staple was ordained. With each film the swarm of villains came in increasingly hellish reconfigurations of the social order, ravenous for power and fuel, fascistic, toxic, yet functional. And homoerotic.

Slender as a branch beneath a jagged crop of midnight-black hair trimmed by hand, Moriceau had been one of Malcolm McClaren's crew of provocateurs who set up shop on London's King's Road in the mid-seventies. She specialised in giving vintage biker gear an S&M slant, ironic infusions of violent motifs, pure bad taste, and had dressed Johnny Rotten and Sid Vicious. In 1981, the reverberations of punk could still be felt. Even in Australia.

> "GIVEN ENOUGH TIME, PEOPLE, NO MATTER HOW IMPOVERISHED, WILL HAVE AN EYE FOR BEAUTY."
>
> – GEORGE MILLER

ABOVE: Coitus very much interruptus – two of Humungus's clan have their moment of passion forestalled when their tent is blown away. It is a rare sighting of sexual activity in the barren future, and a nod to *Mad Max*'s Ozploitation DNA.

OPPOSITE: *Mad Max 2*'s famous array of wacky racers were commissioned at $3000 (Australian) a car. An aesthetic logic was established for the saga – the cars were a response to the environment and built from anything they could lay their hands on. There was also an element of Hollywood parody.

Miller held to a theory that art would endure in the direst of circumstances and among the direst of people: "Given enough time, people, no matter how impoverished, will have an eye for beauty." Punk's scrapyard aesthetic, repurposing old motifs, was the natural form of expression for his post-apocalyptic tribes. Fashion fashioned from the past. Visual rock 'n' roll.

With the demise of punk, Moriceau, a child of Wollongong, New South Wales, returned home and found work in the Sydney film scene making outback period costumes for the New Wave. Amusingly, she would one day dress *Crocodile Dundee*. But *Mad Max 2* and *Thunderdome* remain her defining work – just as she was one of the defining artists of a world where characters double as set decoration – a mode she classified as "male trouble" or "big butch business." It was a parody of masculinity. Poor health limited her involvement in *Fury Road* (Moriceau died in 2016), but successor Jenny Bevan was presented with boxes of recycled rags, soldered metal, and the best of Sydney's S&M boutiques accumulated in readiness for a return to the deviant future.

Does the charge of homophobia stick? From the very first, the *Mad Max* films fostered an aura of camp. Roger Ward, *Mad Max*'s chief of police, Fifi Macaffee, is seen topless in leather

pants and scarf. Toecutter's marauding goons corner a young couple and rape both. The sequel is unabashed. Wez has a pretty blonde boy, Golden Youth (Jerry O'Sullivan), on the end of a chain. The writing team, channelling an increasingly arcane lexicon of mutated Aussie slang, referred in the script to Gayboy Bezerkers and Smegma Crazies. In the later films the camp, while still present, hardens into a landlocked piratical code and a quasi-religious exoticism.

Miller rationalised the sexuality of his films in dystopian terms. In the melting pot of this primitive future, there would be little time for recreational sex. It is unlikely a pregnant woman or child would survive (a theme central to *Fury Road*). He foresaw a drift into homosexual relationships. There was no longer a distinction. Social stigmas were gone with society. During the writing process, genders fluctuated. "Men and women were simply interchangeable," he said. Golden Youth had begun as a female; Virginia Hay's Warrior Woman had started as a man.

Could it simply be that these films are unapologetically kinky?

There had been a plan to cast Ward in the sequel, instituting a surreal tradition of actors returning in different roles. But Ward had been maddened by Miller's request that he audition. Miller attempted to mollify his old friend.

"Fifi! Come in and tell me a joke."

He was experimenting with a new casting technique. A prospective actor didn't read lines from the script but told him an off-the-cuff joke – in effect, a perfectly formed story. Ward began with his punchline.

"Fifty grand!" he announced.

That's how much he wanted to appear in the sequel. A furious Miller threw him out of his office, and they didn't speak for a decade.

"YOU'RE A SCAVENGER, MAX. YOU'RE A MAGGOT. DID YOU KNOW THAT? YOU'RE LIVING OFF THE CORPSE OF THE OLD WORLD."
– PAPPAGALLO

Gibson's Max is apocalyptically deadpan, but there is a comic vein that runs through the film. Humungus and his minions are lethal but consciously absurd. And The Gyro Captain, played by the lanky, lively Spence in yellow long johns, is the film's court jester – and ultimately an ally of sorts to Max. The Auckland-born Spence, a frequent presence in the early days of the New Wave, caught on to Miller's antic auditioning process by improvising crazy routines. He and Miller would reason that back before the collapse The Gyro Captain was some kind of slippery used car salesman.

"He could be genteel, you know," said Spence. "He had his habits."

Spence is now a genre institution, celebrated for having lent his hatstand physique and eccentric delivery to major franchises: *Star Wars*, *The Matrix*, *The Lord of the Rings*. But his presence in *Mad Max* made him iconic – as a kind of inverse of Max: jabbering,

PREVIOUS SPREAD: Max at the wheel of his original V8 Ford Falcon XB GT Interceptor, black on black. The model was brought out of retirement from the first film to be used for close-ups, with a stunt version used for the hard stuff.

OPPOSITE: Three pale-clad warriors of The Compound, William Zappa, David Slingsby, and Virginia Hey as the Warrior Woman. Gibson appreciated how the film was perfectly willing to dispense with a potential love interest for Max in the Warrior Woman.

OPPOSITE BELOW: The Gyro Captain, digging out the remains of a can of Dinki-Di. The blackly comic sight of humans eagerly consuming dog food was a stark reminder of what is at stake.

BELOW: Like Max and his feral dog, the snake is an extension of The Gyro Captain's slippery nature.

OPPOSITE: Emil Minty as The Feral Kid, catching his steel boomerang. The weapon embodied the film's ethos – Australian culture redefined with a cutting edge.

ABOVE: The eight-year-old Minty came out to the desert having done no more than a commercial and spent three months running about in furs, the dirtier the better, having the time of his life.

opportunistic, uncool. He wears his madness on the outside. Nicholas Hoult's Nox in *Fury Road* is infused with similar traits.

What gives *Mad Max 2* its truculent heart is The Feral Kid (Emil Minty): a guttural foundling with a mullet, who brandishes a razor-edged boomerang and latches on to Max, an echo of the son the road warrior has lost. He is halfway to an animal (an extension of Max's dog), inspired by street urchins in Vietnam, said Miller, orphans growing up on the streets of Saigon, half-American and half-Vietnamese. "To them a brutal world was the natural state. Yet they were still children. They still had the innocence." And according to Miller's looking-glass redrafting of *Shane*, he slots into the part of Brandon deWilde's hero-worshipping Joey.

"It was wild for an eight-year-old," remembered Minty, who had been signed up to a Sydney agency and done no more than a lemonade commercial. He had no idea what he was getting into: three months in furs, coached each day, first by his mother, then Miller, and often Gibson, then strapped to a safety harness to cling to the bonnet of a moving truck. "I don't remember being scared." At the end of the film, it becomes clear that the film's stern narrator (voiced by Harold Baigent) is The Feral Kid, who has survived to grow old.

"On the roads it was a white-line nightmare."

They shot through the bitter winter of 1981. While they had more money, they had less time. Release dates were set, the clock ticking. Expectation becomes a driving force. Such was the price of success.

Anyone who laid eyes on Miller said the same thing. He didn't look like the director of *Mad Max*. A little overweight, pipe in hand, fountain of curly black hair, and a handlebar moustache framing an uneasy smile, he resembled a genial sociology professor bemused to find himself orchestrating mayhem. When the wind picked up he wrapped his head in a scarf like a sultan. But the beatific exterior belied the whirring gears beneath. How his mind ticked as he sought that vision within: measuring his film in seconds, pieces of action that would slot together to form a story. He had watched *The General* again and again: Buster Keaton's silent masterpiece, made in cinema's infancy, with its runaway trains. Still thrilling to how it all been done in camera.

"IT WAS WILD FOR AN EIGHT-YEAR-OLD ... I DON'T REMEMBER BEING SCARED."

– EMIL MINTY

Miller now accepted that happenstance was a part of filmmaking, but he was determined to gain a semblance of the control he had lacked on the original. That meant "storyboarding everything." Stunts were broken down into their components, the atoms of individual shots, and a cartoonist was hired to sketch sequences like panels in a comic book. Miller perceived a science.

"You never really see a whole stunt from beginning to end in this movie, or in most movies. You see individual shots, each one carefully planned and safely executed, which when they're edited together, create the illusion of a dangerous stunt." This was the Maxist dialectic.

How ironic it was that a director so determined to hold tight to the filmmaking reins would be drawn to envisage a world of chaos. This involved two hundred stunts,

ABOVE: Mel Gibson would help coach the Emil Minty through the often complex action sequences. Among fans, a theory abides that Tom Hardy's version of the lead character from *Fury Road* is The Feral Kid grown up.

OPPOSITE: Max at the wheel of the tanker that would become one the central motifs of the saga. With twenty gears, the Mack R600 Cool Power was a devil to drive.

ABOVE: Wes (or at least the stunt Wells) in full flight. By the second film, director George Miller had strategised his approach to stunts, breaking each sequence down into constituent shots. The result is precisely orchestrated mayhem.

OPPOSITE: The wild Wez attempts to take revenge on The Feral Kid for the slaying of his pet Golden Youth (Jerry O'Sullivan). The film hovers gleefully on the edge of violent camp.

a crew of one hundred and forty, forty cast, and eighty handmade vehicles. Production designer Graham "Grace" Walker sat in on the storyboarding sessions and was encouraged to contribute his own ideas as they brainstormed their future-retro world, wallpapering the room with their screwball concoctions. Design had to serve action; logic had to serve design. Why do things look this way? It was a process of layering. How would they get at the oil? "How about they have one of those old oil pumps?" suggested Walker. The things you saw in a gas station. Bingo. Put that down.

Fleets of transporters took the long road from Sydney to Broken Hill laden with every manner of contraption. Passing through isolated towns, locals would line the roads to watch the future roll by. Miller, and especially Kennedy, wanted the vehicles to match the clothes: madcap bone bags on wheels assembled at $3,000 a car. The theory was simple – the road warriors would build and maintain their vehicles using whatever they could lay their hands on. They were further examples of Miller's school of post-apocalyptic artistic expression: scavenger memorials, mobile sculptures, characters in their own right. Humungus's six-wheeler was equipped with bull horns, cowhide seat and a speaker system. There was a Ford chassis under there

somewhere. Pappagallo's moon buggy was built from scratch with an engine at either end. Art imitating fiction, it was repurposed for *Thunderdome*. On they went, out into the desert, where the open road awaited them.

"I made a point of getting really the best possible crew we could find," said Miller. He shuddered at the memory of the television vets he was lumbered with on the original, so short-sighted, unable to figure out where he was going. "I think this was Dean Semler's second feature and his attitude was, give anything a go – it's crazy but give it a go, we'll back you all the way."

As cinematographer, Semler had never shot action before. He had come from news reports and documentaries. Which helped. He came at their road wars with an eye for the clear, natural light of the outback. Wide shots, aerials, those great Australian vistas, then zooming in like a cartoon for close-ups. "You could see forever," he marvelled, "like fifty miles." There was just sky and road. For that vital sense of speed: low-slung cameras fitted with wide-angled lenses, inches from the bitumen. All things Miller had learned on *Mad Max* but better. The chaos had a clarity.

Miller and Kennedy still conferred like brothers, but it was clearer now who was director and who was producer. They shot in

OPPOSITE: Max makes his point with the legendary if unreliable sawn-off shotgun. With the aid of cinematographer Dean Semler, George Miller gave the film an epic texture worthy of the Western giants John Ford or Sergio Leone.

BELOW: Max had also evolved to quite deliberately echo Clint Eastwood's unsmiling gunslinger The Man with No Name, drawn across the desert by his own amoral code.

continuity, first scene to last. It was another way of maintaining control. Microphones were stowed on vehicles to catch the punch of acceleration, the shimmy of gears and the shockwave of collision.

To blow up the compound, Kennedy returned to his contact at the MOD. They brought army engineers to Broken Hill, guys who could lay their hands on real explosives. It was a concert of triggered explosions: the central fireball then a series of incendiaries sending oil drums skyward. They had to stop the flights from Adelaide and warn local mines. The crew

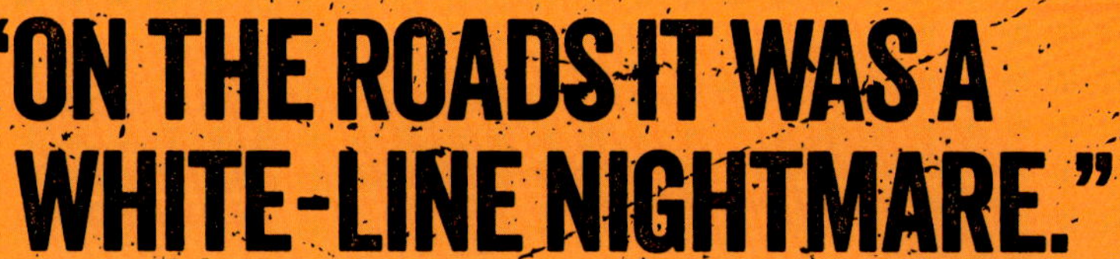

"ON THE ROADS IT WAS A WHITE-LINE NIGHTMARE."

– THE NARRATOR

gathered to watch on a nearby hill. It looked like the end of the world.

The production wouldn't have a clean bill of health. Stunts still went drastically wrong. Chief stuntman Guy Norris (in the guise of Bearclaw Mohawk) simply had to hit an upturned buggy with his bike, launching himself through the air and into a ditch piled with cardboard boxes. They had a name for it: a "cannonball." He had done it dozens of times. But he got his timing wrong, didn't leave the bike before impact, clipping the handlebars. That sent him end-over-end, his body as rigid as a stick; a shockingly unreal sight through the lens. Miller rushed to his side,

serving as set doctor as well as director, fearing the worst. By an ironic miracle, a pin in Norris's femur from a previous break had taken the brunt of the landing, ending up bent at a right angle. Miller used the shot.

Fortunately, Norris wasn't due to roll the truck. That privilege went to a Kenilworth dealer from St. Peters, Sydney, named Dennis Williams, who had never heard of Mel Gibson or *Mad Max*. He had simply sold them the Mack R600 Cool Power they were going to total. A tricky beast, given it had twenty-two gears. So the production hired Williams to drive their truck. It was Hayes who had the idea. Or more of an inkling for how their great chase would reach its crescendo – send the tanker, steered by Max, assailed by Humungus's roaches, rolling off the highway at full speed. Out on the road to Mundi-Mundi, exactly where the film had begun. "Piece of cake," said Williams. Theoretically.

The big rig becomes the central *Max* motif, born out of the tradition of the stagecoach assailed by natives, bandits leaping on trains. In *Thunderdome* it is a Mack on rails chased by the Bartertown hive. By *Fury Road*, the war rig is the setting for the entire film. Nitro-injected, phallic, doomed.

So Williams is at the wheel of an icon in the making. The cab has been stripped of anything that isn't vital, including the windscreen. Anything that could potentially kill him. A roll cage has been assembled. A chain runs down the length of the tanker, preventing it from jack-knifing (just). There is only enough fuel for the downhill run, reducing the chance of going up in flames. At 100 mph, as he hits the bend, the plan is to flip ninety degrees and sprawl into the red earth like a great beast felled by a hunt. Wet

sandbags are packed into the tanker's left-hand side to assist gravity.

Williams pulls out on the first run, his nerves getting the better of him. He takes a breath and goes again. Second time, he sees his mark, wrenches the wheel, there is a brief moment of weightlessness, the world spins off its axis, then impact, chaos, noise, and the cab is engulfed with iron-rich Australian dirt.

"Cut!" shouts Miller.

And they begin running. The entire crew is on the move to get to the wreck and Williams. The smoke clears. A round of applause breaks out – half elation, half relief – as he is seen on his feet, getting his breath, ushering away the paramedics. As Williams begins to walk away his knees buckle.

"I fell to the ground like a bag of shit," he recalled.

The final act of *Mad Max 2* remains one of the most enduring action sequences anywhere in cinema. The guitar solo of Miller's visual rock 'n' roll. Wez sandwiched between vehicles as Humungus hits the tanker head-on, the images syncopated with the gyrocopter's eye-view, swooping over the battle like a hornet. The collision sends the tanker careering off the road. And now comes the punchline. Out of it pours sand, nothing but sand. Max was a decoy, as the good guys slip into the desert with their guzzaline. Of all things, he laughs. Max had to reveal his humanity, a sense of hope, said Hayes, "otherwise what's the point of this world?" All the *Mad Max* sequels return him to the desert. Back to square one. But revived by human contact.

OPPOSITE: Battered but not bowed, Max bears the results of his brush with death. The idea was that the hero would always look as battered as the vehicles. A former doctor, George Miller was a stickler for accurate make-up.

BELOW: A superstar emerges from the wreckage – Gibson was already on his way to Hollywood, but *Mad Max 2* would confirm his growing status among the studio dealmakers. But Max will always exemplify his Australian roots.

The arrival of *Mad Max 2* is still reverberating today. A new age of thrilling, cinematic barbarism had come. Themes only hinted at in the original were fully expressed in the sequel. These were antiheroic times, the timeworn genres have been recombined, assembled from the remnants of the old order into something aggressively new. "Miller keeps the eye alert, the mind agitated, the Saturday-matinee spirit alive," wrote Richard Corliss in *Time*. Max was the man with one thousand ironies (Miller's film is literally post-modern). It was another worldwide smash, this time including America, with $36 million on its initial release.

All the fuss over Maxian violence had noticeably quieted. It was the nature of the first film that caught the flak, said Miller. The tone. "Because the second was more optimistic and a bit cartoony, there wasn't so much." *Mad Max* had almost become respectable.

After triumph comes tragedy. A devastating footnote. On the winter's afternoon of 17 July 1983, Kennedy was at the controls of his Bell JetRanger helicopter, taking a pleasure trip alongside fifteen-year-old family friend Victor Evatt, flying south of Sydney. Coming in too low over Lake Burragorang in the Blue Mountains, the skids broke the surface of the icy water and Kennedy, an expert pilot, lost control. A search plane found them the next morning – Evatt had spelled out "help" with rocks – but Kennedy had died during the night, a combination of a broken back and freezing temperatures. He was thirty-three. Miller knew there could be no more *Mad Max*.

THUNDER

DOME

"DEATH IS LISTENING, AND WILL TAKE THE FIRST MAN THAT SCREAMS."

– AUNTY ENTITY

At Coober Pedy the heat was insane. The mercury regularly climbed above fifty degrees Celsius. It was so hot, the film melted inside the cameras. It was so dry, the crew were coughing up blood. And the infernal dust, whipped up by the infernal wind, jammed cameras and clogged engines. It was like making a film during the apocalypse. The studs and buckles of Norma Moriceau's latest line in dystopian chic would leave livid burn marks on flesh. The consumption of alcohol had been (ineffectually) banned by the good Doctor Miller. Less to keep his production in line than to limit dehydration. Cast and crew had stopped urinating. Liquids simply evaporated from their skin. Fuel would vaporise before it hit the tank.

PREVIOUS SPREAD: Planes, trains, and some kind of automobiles – *Mad Max Thunderdome* boasted every mode of transport yet is the most restrained of all the films.

OPPOSITE: Mild Max – one of the chief disappointments for core fans was Mel Gibson's shift from nihilistic antihero to saviour figure, rescuing this lost tribe of children.

The only respite came below ground. The name, Coober Pedy, derives from the Aboriginal *kupa piti*, which translates to "white man's holes." The local sandstone had been riddled with mines in search of opals. Burrowed "dugouts" remained the main form of housing. The town, if you want to call it that, was over five hundred miles from Adelaide, halfway to Alice Springs on the everlasting Stuart Highway, in the Great Victoria Desert of South Australia.

In November 1984, at the height of summer, the strange community that had congregated there like a remote tribe, a collection of strays, vagabonds and artists, with their own outré set of

ABOVE: George Miller, oblivious to the heat in an orange top, frames a shot of the children in the Crack in the Earth, in fact, the Mermaid's Cave Gorge in the Blue Mountains …

OPPOSITE TOP: … Miller (with Mel Gibson on the Bartertown set in Sydney) would share directing duties on the third *Mad Max* with George Ogilvie …

OPPOSITE: … Ogilvie and Miller survey the scene together. Nominally, Ogilvie would handle the performances and Miller the visuals and action, but there is no doubt that Miller's unique style dominates.

customs, found their peace shattered by an even stranger tribe: mohawks and baldies, kids in caveman furs, and if their eyes did not deceive them, Tina Turner wearing what looked like fine grey chain mail, because that is exactly what it was. For five burning weeks, their desert outpost was the location for both the beginning and end of a third *Mad Max* film, with Mel Gibson still encased in the worn leathers and icy glower of the cult hero. Coober Pedy is where finally the cars will roll, buzzing like wasps, for the frenetic, emblematic, custom-built George Miller chase sequence.

There is still sand, still rock, a landscape as barren as the surface of the Moon, but the textures of *Mad Max Beyond Thunderdome* are noticeably different from what has come before. In the shadow of Kennedy's passing, Miller was in even more philosophical mood. With the exception of Max's Camel Wagon, which conceals a Ford F-150 chassis mounted with a Ford XA sedan cab (a Frankensteinian off-roader if he had any gas), and a light aircraft piloted by an oddball named Jedediah, who has an oddly familiar face given it belongs to Bruce Spence, there isn't a single moving vehicle until the third act. This was a radical rethink of Maxian principles. *Thunderdome* is still considered the weakest of the *Mad Max* films, but there is no question it is the most ambitious.

In the wake of *Mad Max 2*'s success, Byron Kennedy had speculated that *Mad Max 3* would need to take a progressive step deeper into science fiction, with Max found among the ruins of Sydney, the great shipwreck of civilisation, glimpsed briefly in the eventual third film's coda.

For months, Miller couldn't face the idea of making the third film without his partner. It felt like a betrayal. Yet the story would not be denied. Recalling "the most intense working period" of his life (until *Fury Road*), he found that returning to the future was a way of mourning his best friend. Backed by Warner Brothers, this was in effect a Hollywood movie. Not that the sun-baked Australian crew paid heed to such niceties. They had a familiar gleam in the eye. Fact and fiction began blurring again. One of *Thunderdome*'s wolfpack of mechanics gained a reputation for eating live cockroaches to order. A security guard was cast after he was spotted juggling knives on his tea breaks. Within the production, it was the usual madness. Except for the fact that the studio were providing an unprecedented $12 million to discover the whereabouts of the popular antihero. Miller could afford to dream big.

He and an eager Terry Hayes had met up in Los Angeles (times were indeed changing) to complete a trilogy of films. As was his wont, Miller began by discussing quantum mechanics. "The theory of the oscillating universe," recalled Hayes. The director's oblique thought process became the springboard to the question of what shape a third *Mad Max* film might take. Ninety minutes later they had a story mapped out. Max's universe was oscillating.

The third part is set fifteen years after the events of the previous one. But the future is retreating deeper into the past. More than Broken Hill, this was a vision of the hardscrabble interior that greeted settlers and convicts: a desert land, Biblically bleak, where the first lesson was survival. Here Miller let his myths roam, reaching for mystical connections, an epic framework, a grander dystopia.

Hayes posited a theory that those who are short on knowledge tend to be big on belief. That stirred something in Miller. Was this how religions were born? "If you take the Aboriginal tribes of Australia," he said, "they just take simple empirical information and using those little bits of the jigsaw construct very elaborate mystical beliefs, which explain the

"FOR MONTHS, MILLER COULDN'T FACE THE IDEA OF MAKING THE THIRD FILM WITHOUT HIS PARTNER."

whole universe." Their script moved between two opposing worlds: the adult clamour and corruption of methane-powered Bartertown (science) and the ethereal, deluded, childlike Eden of The Crack in the Earth (religion). Caught between them – Max.

"There *would* have been no point in doing it again if it was gonna be the same thing," insisted Gibson, interviewed on set, looking ever more the movie star. "However, it isn't. I think George and Terry are getting better as they go along. They've actually taken the whole *Max* concept a step further." Gone, he reflected, was the relentless violence of the first, and

> **"THERE WOULD HAVE BEEN NO POINT IN DOING IT AGAIN IF IT WAS GONNA BE THE SAME THING."**
>
> – MEL GIBSON

ABOVE: Max (Mel Gibson) shielded from the desert wearing a classic Arabian keffiyeh, in Maxian black, of course. George Miller was purposefully reaching for a *Lawrence of Arabia* vibe with the third film.

LEFT: Max at the wheel – the car stunts would come in the third act, but the film was attempting to show the world a stage further into the post-apocalyptic future, with civilisation attempting to grow roots.

OPPOSITE: The Gyro Captain-reborn – Jedediah (Bruce Spence, right) and son (Adam Cockburn) subsist quite successfully, pilfering on the margins until Max shows up.

the stylised, more clownish approach of the second. "Oh, it had that hard feeling – so will this one. But now it's going from that toward . . . well, something perhaps a bit more hopeful."

The film opens not with the snarl of an engine, but a bird's-eye view of a vast plain, the curve of a dried-out riverbed like a petrified road. It's a shot worthy of David Lean. The great, bleak desert epic *Lawrence of Arabia* was on Miller's mind. Something grandiose. A shift in mode heightened by the hiring of *Lawrence*-composer Maurice Jarre to give the score some romantic pep (as well as a chorus of anvils). Gibson took to referring to his director as "Cecil B. DeMiller." The encircling perspective turns out to be the view from a Transavia PL-12 Airtruk "Flying Jalopy," and Jedediah and son (a spiky little snot played by Adam Cockburn in matching pith helmet) are homing in on their quarry – a caravan of camels (as bad tempered as any of the cast), kicking up dust in the distance. The owner will prove to be Max, clutching the reins of the Camel Wagon, shielded in a keffiyeh. Swept from his perch by the swooping aircraft, he is left sprinting after his stolen belongings.

The scene was shot 9 miles north of Coober Pedy in a place known as The Breakaways, but to the Aboriginal peoples these were the plains of Kata Tjuta. Seeking permission to film on sacred ground, location manager Graham Maddix and Miller appealed to the Pitjantjatjara tribal elders. This required a translator given the elders spoke no English. Sat on the ground, Miller narrated the plot of the third *Mad Max*, just as he had pitched it

to the elders at Warner. To his surprise, his hosts got quite worked up. When it was clear he had come to the end, they began to dance. This was their way of granting the director permission to film on the great red shelf of Kata Tjuta. As they explained to an awestruck Miller, they had heard his tale before. This was one of their stories.

In his 1997 documentary, *40,000 Years of Dreaming*, Miller goes in search of the origins of storytelling, his abiding fascination. He presents his findings himself, a soft-spoken shaman. Joseph Campbell figures, of course. Central is the idea that story crosses geographical and temporal boundaries. A vast interconnectivity lies between all works of art, all films. The Dreaming, as Aboriginal peoples referred to it, saw no difference between past, present and future.

Thunderdome's plot is the most convoluted of all the *Mad Max* films, divided into three separate acts in three different locations. The first third sustains the same raucous spirit as its predecessor. With one major difference. The roving cutthroats are now of fixed abode – the resplendently filthy Bartertown. "Helping build a better future" proclaims a wooden sign on Max's arrival, the camera craning over the gateway in tribute to Sergio Leone's introduction to Flagstone in *Once Upon a Time in the West*. Beyond is an imaginative leap that is pure Miller. Constructed in the Homebush State Brickworks, the oldest working brick factory in Australia, in other

words a dust-smogged quarry on the edge of Sydney, Bartertown is Deadwood painted by Hieronymus Bosch, a leprous Moss Eisley literally powered by pig shit. "All the juice is now gone," explained Gibson. Miller and Hayes shift the power source from petroleum to methane.

The filmmaking methodology was changing too. With money at his disposal, Miller could build his world on a scale unimaginable to the young man who had relied upon Melbourne's corroded hinterlands as a backdrop. His recycled aesthetic was applied to an entire town, the biggest set ever built in Australia (also house style). Three hundred extras milled through this monument to post-apocalyptic dun, a sprawling shantytown given a final weathering by set decorator Martin O'Neill with the aid of a pump-action shotgun. At ninety degrees, Sydney was merely unbearable compared to Coober Pedy.

Miller was going big on animals: camels, goats, dogs, and especially pigs. The smell was ripe. And shooting even more of a trial. Max's latest companion is a shrill and resourceful capuchin. In real life, a monkey by the name of Sally Ann who behaved impeccably until the cameras rolled and she just jumped up and down on the spot in frustration. "We had to grab any shot we could," sighed Hayes.

It is evident that a rough-hewn stability has been established; the kind of order-out-of-chaos autocracy of the American frontier. Bartertown is presided over by Turner's Aunty Entity from the relative comfort of her penthouse. Miller sought a rock 'n' roll charisma for his key villain, combined with a female energy to set the role apart from the masculine mania of Toecutter and Humungus. She was to be a regal figure, a queen at court. "Someone like Tina Turner," he kept saying to Hayes.

ABOVE: The eternal realist – a forlorn Mel Gibson and friend, the often uncooperative capuchin Sally Ann, take a moment. The increase in animal performers would be another self-imposed trial for George Miller.

OPPOSITE: Older but still the warrior – a publicity shot of the iconic Max wearing the same jacket and clutching the same shotgun (though his guns are hardly called upon). The film is set fifteen years after *Mad Max 2*.

"I BUILT A LIFE AFTER MY DIVORCE. SHE BUILT A TOWN."

– TINA TURNER

ABOVE: For the chief villain, the shimmering Aunty Entity, George Miller wanted a rock star vibe – he had expected that Tina Turner wouldn't agree, but she didn't think twice about leaping into the future.

OPPOSITE: Aunty's look was pure medieval-futurism – a fine chainmail dress made from soldered coat hangers and chicken wire. She represented a form of progress souring with power.

The Tennessee-born, Grammy-winning singer was an American institution: ten million albums sold, global tours, the iconic survivor of a tumultuous and abusive marriage to musical partner Ike Turner. Beyond a cameo in the rock opera *Tommy*, she had shown little interest in movies, turning down Spielberg's *The Color Purple*. Too depressing. Then she shocked everyone, including Miller, by leaping at the chance to make a *Mad Max* movie. "I'll do it!" she roared down the phone. Without a trace of diva-like behaviour, den-mother to the eccentric crew, she threw herself into the hardships of a *Mad Max* shoot, catching vibrations of her own story in this striking survivor she was playing.

"I built a life after my divorce. She built a town."

"Aunty," as she is known, is an ambiguous creature.

"One of the main reasons we cast Tina Turner is that she's perceived as being a fairly positive persona. You don't think of Tina Turner as someone dark," said Miller.

Aunty is ruthless. That's the point. But according to Miller also an "agent of evolution." Heroes of the revolution are tomorrow's tyrants as the saying goes. She is a self-made queen. A nobody who became a somebody. "So much for history," she quips to Max, brandishing a mane of long, blonde hair, perfect Hollywood teeth (Bartertown must have good dental) and an unforgettable range of dystopian bling. Moriceau's chain-mail dress, gloves and stockings were made from seventy lbs of soldered coat hangers and chicken wire. Critics were quick to praise the zip Turner gave to a dense film. "Explosive, pungent, bigger than life," enthused the *Los Angeles Times*. "A genuine actress and not just a curiosity piece," claimed the *Chicago Tribune*.

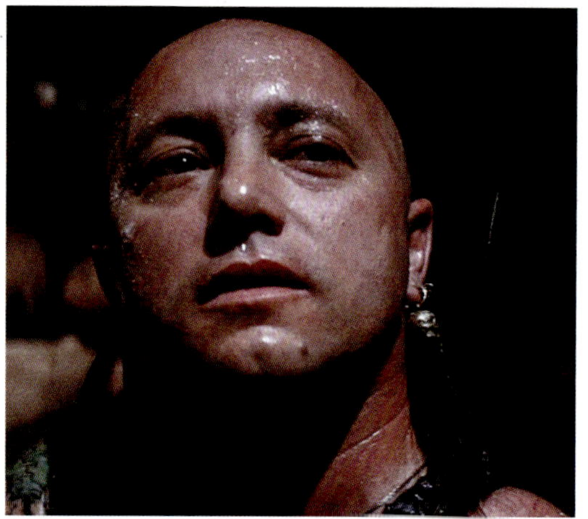

PREVIOUS SPREAD: Aunty Entity goes on tour – *Thunderdome*'s road wars were filmed at Cooper Pedy where it was so hot the petrol would evaporate before it hit the tank.

TOP: A role call of oddballs: Aunty's accountant The Collector (classical actor Frank Thring) strikes a bargain with a long-haired Max ...

ABOVE LEFT: ... Australian rock star Angry Anderson as Aunty's chief heavy Ironbar, who doesn't have a line ...

ABOVE RIGHT: ... Aunty and Max survey the proto-civilisation of Bartertown ...

OPPOSITE: ... Brains and brawn – Master (Angelo Rossitto) commands Bartertown's Underworld perched on the shoulders of Blaster (Paul Larsson), his gargantuan bodyguard.

Aunty's mob are a familiar freakshow. The capacity of Miller's rabble of stunties in mohawk head-dresses to startle was waning. That said, as Bartertown's corpulent accountant The Collector, Frank Thring brought some classical pedigree. Once a travelling conjuror in the outback, he was the first Australian to make professional sound pictures, before flourishing in bona fide Hollywood epics. Thring played Pontius Pilate in *Ben-Hur* and Herod in *King of Kings*, and made a vivid impression in *The Vikings* and *El Cid*. He had that kind of face, that kind of voice – a cold grandeur ready-made for history's schemers – and remarkable soft, blue eyes.

Angry Anderson brought a different energy. Bad boy frontman of blues-metal outfit Rose Tattoo, a cult figure in Australia, the

Melbourne-born Anderson (real name Gary) ostensibly fills the Vernon Wells role. He's the new Wez. Without a single line, Ironbar is a blend of silent comedy and *Looney Tunes*, working his way through a cat's quota of lives. Stocky, hairless, inked to the gills, Anderson was halfway to the *Max* already.

"I fell in love with *Mad Max*, tragically, from the first movie," he confessed. He didn't much care for films, but he cared about *Mad Max*, pursuing a role as soon as a sequel was announced. Luckily, this was Australia. He and Miller were mates.

Aunty has a proposition for Max – his camels, his truck and precious methane in return for killing her arch-rival Master Blaster. For there is a power struggle underway in Bartertown. Old habits die hard. King of the Underworld (things are getting Greek), the engine room of Bartertown, Master Blaster turns out to be a double act. Master, a dwarf (Angelo Rossitto had featured in the 1932 *Freaks*, *The Wizard of Oz* and a battalion of Hollywood B-pictures), is the brains of the outfit. He alone knows the trick of turning pig excrement into energy. And Blaster (Paul Larsson), his hulking bodyguard, is the muscle, carrying Master on his shoulders, his head concealed in a diver's helmet.

The four hundred pigs that populate the Underworld – in fact, a bull ring in Glebe, Sydney – were the subject of their own saga. The production was taken to the High Court on the suspicion their roving pig farm was a hotbed for transmissible diseases. The City of Sydney made wild claims that pig urine could jump two feet into the air and be absorbed into the atmosphere. Such were the foibles of *Mad Max* making. The production had to guarantee that the pigs were comfortably housed beneath air filters and deodorisers. Miller's enthusiasm for his swinish cast members (who only kicked

OPPOSITE: Two men enter, one man leaves – Max battles it out in the iconic Thunderdome, part gladiatorial arena, part gameshow, part small claims court.

OPPOSITE BELOW: The man in the ironic mask – for all his strength Blaster will turn out to be far less of the warrior than advertised.

BELOW: The concept of the Thunderdome, this geodesic battleground, has transcended the film to enter pop culture as the ultimate one-on-one competitive test.

up a stink when *not* required on set) would evolve into *Babe*.

It's Blaster who must die, says Aunty, but the semblance of law must be maintained. Time for another edition of Thunderdome. Providing the film with its subtitle, Miller's most original and thrilling advance on Maxian mythology is a gladiatorial arena wherein differences between the citizenry of Bartertown are resolved. By fighting to the death. "Two men enter!" comes the rhythmic chorus of the crowd. "One man leaves!" Each contestant is strapped to elastic cords hanging from the ceiling, allowing them to leap and pirouette around the dome, reaching for strategically placed spears or chainsaws and avoiding the iron spikes. As a child, Miller put serious and practical thought into how he might fly like Superman. Did he imagine attaching vast elastic bands to his waist, pulling them taut, then letting go? This fabulous, deranged, acrobatic duel redefines the fight sequence just as *Mad Max 2* revolutionises the car chase. An entire dystopia is compressed into a hemispheric wooden cage swathed in the heaving bodies of the mob.

"We wanted to account for entertainment," said Miller, who reasoned that even the lowlifes of Bartertown would want to redirect aggression. "We thought wouldn't it be great,

TOP: George Miller's brilliant thematic concept was that the entire world of *Mad Max* was contained within the Thunderdome - there may be no cars involved, but it was still a matter of negotiating momentum, braking and collisions, as the contestants are launched on spring-loaded cables.

ABOVE: Deal gone bad – Ironbar and Dr. Dealgood (Edwin Hodgeman) exile Max to the desert when having refused to kill Blaster. It is the first step in the rebirth of Max's conscience.

OPPOSITE TOP: The iron lady speaks – Aunty Entity lays down the law before the Thunderdome's avid audience. Turner would locate more moral complexities in her character than any other *Mad Max* villain.

OPPOSITE: Not enough runway – Jedediah contends they don't have enough room to get airborne. Thus Max will have to make his messianic sacrifice to clear a path for the getaway plane.

instead of people going to war, they'd fight it out in the Thunderdome." This also provided a form of theatre. Throughout history (not least in film), death has been at the heart of entertainment, and Miller imbued this ritual night out with the pageantry of law courts and churches, the antics of a circus, and the gurning polish of a gameshow. "It was all those things combined," he laughed. Pure Maxian mix and match.

Proceedings are hosted by Edwin Hodgeman as Dr. Dealgood in gigantic shoulder pads and gothic caricature of Joel Grey from *Cabaret*, a film set in Berlin as the Nazi tribe brutalised the streets. In lieu of the voiceover of *Mad Max 2*, there is an outbreak of speechifying: reams of history, rules, warnings and exposition delivered in Miller's singsong jargon like the weaving of enchantments. "Justice is only a roll of the dice. A flip of the coin," eulogises the wizardly Dr. Dealgood. In giggly tribute, he introduces Max as "The Man With No Name." Confirmation that this is post-apocalyptic Spaghetti.

Like the jerry-built language, there are eerie doublings, doppelgangers, repetitions, echoes and visual rhymes that cross borders with the other films. Miller insisted that Spence's Jedediah was a new character. Fans have read him as The Gyro Captain under a new name. They are both pilots. Both oddballs. Is this a Miller twin thing? A mythical recurrence? A mutant sequel? It's as if everyone's roles are preordained. The actors may differ, but George Spartels as Blackfinger, the Underworld's mechanic, is the same character as Steven J. Spears's Mechanic in *Mad Max 2* and David Cameron's Underground Mechanic in *Mad Max*. Greasers all (and one) delivering their worrisome prognosis like Scotty under the bonnet of the *Enterprise*.

In arguably the strangest sequence in a very strange set of films, Max encounters another tribe out in the desert, who have established a proto-civilisation in an oasis within a narrow canyon called The Crack in the Earth. Only there is not an adult to be seen. They are an expansion of The Feral Kid into an entire community of orphans.

OPPOSITE: A publicity shot of Max and four of the feral youngsters he must lead through the desert. Clockwise from the left: Anna Goanna (Justine Clarke), Savannah Nix (Helen Buday), Mr. Skyfish (Mark Spain), and Eddie (Shane Tickner).

BELOW: With the Lost Tribe, George Miller was calling upon the tradition of survivalist children from *Peter Pan*'s Lost Boys to *The Lord of the Flies* to Russell Hoban's *Riddley Walker*.

Max and the kids. This is what still irks the purists. But children have always been on his mind. Tormented by the loss of his child in the first film. Stirred by the devotion of The Feral Kid in the second. Now in the third, he is burdened with saving these castaways and by extension restoring some kind of hope for the future. By *Fury Road* the wacky kids have transformed into the gobby brides, but Max is still in the rescue business. He is always perceived through innocent eyes.

"THIS IS REALLY A STORY ABOUT MAX COMING OUT OF THE CLOSET."

– GEORGE MILLER

But fans and critics thought Miller had gone soft on them. Maybe he had. The Lost Tribe had been at the heart of the initial discussions. "So it automatically had a softer heart to it," acknowledged Miller. Gibson, he laughed, often described Max as a closet human being. Being human wasn't conducive to survival. "And we said, well this is really a story about Max coming out of the closet."

The idea had branched out from the backstory they gave to Emil Minty for The Feral Kid: how he had been in a light aircraft that

landed in the desert, and his dad had gone in search of fuel, never to return. And his mum had gone to find his dad . . . The feral band think Max is the returning Captain Walker, the jet pilot who raced the "pox-clipse" before crashing in the sand. Who went off with the other adults to find help, promising one day to return.

The inference takes shape. The nihilism retreats. His heart heavy with the absence of Kennedy, Miller found a hopeful note amid the Darwinian brutality. He pulled from children's literature. These are the Lost Boys (and Girls) of *Peter Pan* awaiting their ageless captain. And haven't we already seen Max fly in the Thunderdome, attached to wires like a principal boy?

Symbolically, the production found their idyll in the Mermaids Cave, a sandstone cave in the Blue Mountains of New South Wales, the most tranquil portion of filmmaking on any *Mad Max*. Already the father of three (including twin sons), Gibson was enchanted by the company of the forty children picked from 1,800 hopefuls, the best dancers, musicians and gymnasts. "Within ten minutes he was just one of them," laughed Miller. They immediately accepted him. So he was banished from the workshops. They needed him to be stranger – their first encounter with parental authority.

Miller would find himself seeking Kennedy's approval or advice, only to be reminded that he was gone. He later mentioned feeling distracted, unsettled, maybe haunted. Which is why he brought in George Ogilvie to co-direct the film. The idea being that Ogilvie would work with the actors, leaving Miller to concentrate on action and setting. Swept up in those inner visions, Miller can be an enigmatic guide to actors hoping to discuss motivation. Gibson still had to remind himself it wasn't personal: "One day I thought he was being really cruel.

ABOVE: Messianic Max – against his better judgment Max must re-embrace fatherhood in the third film. George Miller was in mythical mode as it becomes Max's destiny to save the future.

OPPOSITE: The aptly named Scrooloose (Rod Zuanic) might look familiar – his black-eyed, pale-faced look was the basis for the War Boys in *Mad Max: Fury Road*.

I thought, 'How could he be so callous?' It's not callousness. It's just that his mind is so directed that you could drive nails through his feet and he would not feel it."

Born in Goulburn, New South Wales, and oddly enough another twin, Ogilvie was celebrated as a director of theatre, ballet and opera. He had got to know Miller directing episodes of Kennedy Miller's successful ventures into television *The Dismissal* and *Bodyline*. And he was nothing if not versatile.

On set in the Blue Mountains in 1984, wearing a sailor's cap and spectacles, and known to gesture with a brolly, Ogilvie holds the attention of his youthful troupe with the air of a slightly irritable choirmaster. He issues stern commands and they follow his every move like a snake charmer.

"Cut," calls Miller, standing beside the camera, as discreet as any man can be wearing a white scarf and hair over his shoulders like Charles II.

"You're just smiling and grinning, don't do anything like that," Ogilvie admonishes his charges, a tableau of caveman chic. "Just make the *sound*. Let's go again."

The Lost Tribe's delivery of "The Tell" of their past, chanting and swaying en masse like Buddhists, is even more bizzare than the junkyard poetics of Bartertown. Hauntingly choreographed by Ogilvie, these are the extremes of Hayes's theory – a belief system made from the scraps of knowledge that have survived the crash. The orphans cling to the ghosts of the past like everyone else in this godforsaken future. The darker hues of *Lord of the Flies* are mixed with the Neverland of *Peter Pan*, and the Chaucerian ("The Miller's Tale"!) prattle of *Riddley Walker*, Russell Hoban's post-nuclear *Huckleberry Finn*. Any

id-stirred violence is reserved for the pirate ship of Bartertown, commanded by their coldly persuasive Captain Hook, Aunty Entity. Grown-ups and children, it's hard to tell the difference.

Miller's storytelling was exploring new possibilities. New idioms. And pursuing a fully redemptive arc for Max. Pushed by Hayes, he went the whole hog – Max the Messiah. Unable to prevent himself from doing the right thing, Max comes to the rescue of a detachment of kids who, disheartened by his inability to raise the wreck of a 747 (the tail shot in lustrous silhouette like an ancient ruin by Dean Semler), have foolishly struck out across the sand for "home." In their number: Savannah Nix (Helen Buday) and Scrooloose (Rod Zuanic), a morbid outcast among outcasts, daubed in white paint and panda eyes, the prototype for the War Boys of *Fury Road*. They are heading straight for Bartertown.

Gibson had his own trials. Offscreen, he struggled with his celebrity. After *Thunderdome*'s release he was the first to be voted Sexiest Man Alive by *People* magazine. *Lethal Weapon* was his next film. It had taken $1.2 million to secure his services. He was now a star of a different order, but wanted to be one of the gang. By his own admission, alcohol was an issue. Onscreen, he delivered another performance of great, minimalist charisma. How this dark world suits him. *Thunderdome* marks the peak of Gibson's poker-faced beauty, his blank expression stirred by flickers of tension, those electric blue eyes always alert. And Max has never been so talkative. He has conversations, albeit quick, terse exchanges. Deals brokered. Truths imparted. The voice of reason in the unreasonable future.

"I think this is a comedy," said Gibson.

"There's a lot to laugh at. George thinks the same." That's their secret code. It's a grim cartoon about the absurdity of humankind. Did he sense that this would be the final time he played Max?

Too quickly and easily Max and his surrogate family pluck the Master from the sewers of Bartertown and flee by rail in a methane-powered 1965 Mack truck modified for the tracks (don't ask when or why). The railway ran to Coober Pedy in single track like the one that bore down on Chinchilla. It was known as The Ghan, from The Afghan Express, named for the Afghani camel drivers who first explored the region. It was surprisingly busy for the middle of nowhere, testing Miller's legendary equanimity as Alice Springs-bound locomotives interrupted filming. They would have to send their train back down the line to make way. Still, the cars had been transported westward by train. For the final act, Miller was getting back to basics. The purity of the chase.

The design policy was the same but less. Under advisement from his director, regular production designer Graham "Grace" Walker theorised that the road warriors were running short on parts, especially bodywork. They were now driving "skeletal" buggies over the gulches of flame-grilled Coober Pedy. Hayes praised the new organic look for the cars. It was "reptilian," he said. It was as if they "had grown out of the environment." They are in hot pursuit of a hybrid train with a cowcatcher spearing the way through a landscape that has no cows. This is Miller's

full homage to *The General*. Ogilvie was nowhere to be seen.

There was a reunion of *Mad Max* vets. Grant Page returned as stunt co-ordinator, Phil Brock as Gibson's stunt driver, with Dennis Williams once again behind the wheel of a Mack, a relatively easier task given it was literally on rails. The automotive cannonade was executed with a seasoned confidence: pipe rolls, full body burns, head-on collisions. Height was the new objective, launching vehicles to grapple in mid-air like the duelling miscreants of the Thunderdome. How far they had come from Kennedy's failed rocket launch. The main concern was the lack of padding on the drivers. It was too hot.

"Normally, in a cool temperature, you pad yourself with wet suits and all sorts of things until you're so well protected that you won't get hurt," said Page. "But out in 146 degrees [Fahrenheit], you can't do that because you'd last three minutes and you'd be dead. We had ten people collapse with exhaustion, and twelve cars collapsed too."

Beyond the heat, Anderson scalding a hand when dry ice leaked from a steaming pipe, and the poor stuntman whose bare foot was trodden on by a horse in Bartertown, there were no serious injuries. Ever game, Turner demanded the chance to drive her own chariot, which required the transmission be repurposed as an automatic. Ambushed by Jedediah and son once more, who provide a getaway plane, Max gets back behind the wheel (finally) to clear the route for take-off. He is left behind. Again. Full circle.

ABOVE LEFT: The line to nowhere – an on-set shot of Max and the youngsters attempt to getaway in a Mack truck on rails being brought to an abrupt stop by Jedediah Jr. (Adam Cockburn) in classic Western tradition.

ABOVE: Wacky racers – by the third film the concept is that the lack of parts has reduced the cars to unrecognizable contraptions, almost like bugs that have scuttled out of the ground.

With distance, Miller was rueful about *Thunderdome*. Maybe his mind wasn't settled. Maybe his heart wasn't right. "The biggest problem was cramming all that information into one hundred minutes," he admitted. Where *Mad Max 2* was streamlined, *Thunderdome* laboured through subplots, backstories, introductions, deeper currents. With the second film, the visceral thrill belied greater meanings. Ideas we would ponder at our leisure. The hows and whys of this "pox-clipse" realm. Morality, decency and hope were whispers on the hot wind.

Without Kennedy there was a danger of Miller getting lost in his mythological layering like a hall of mirrors. He was telling too many stories. *"Mad Max III* is baroque, larded, even cluttered, with incidental detail, and verging on the surreal," said Robert C. Cumbow, summing up the experience in *Slant*. Couldn't it have just told the sordid tale of Bartertown? Did we really need to go beyond Thunderdome? The box office swelled ($36 million worldwide – Max still a universal export), and two hit singles from Turner helped (though were another sign of commercial softening), but the reviews were mixed. Fans look back on it as the weak link.

This is a relative argument. One that compares *Thunderdome* to two of the greatest action films ever made and an electrifying debut. *Thunderdome* may be less than the sum of its parts, but what parts they are: Bartertown, Aunty, the Thunderdome, those weird children, the loony lingo, the scrum-down of bug-like vehicles, the full expressionist vortex of Miller's futurescape. The imprint of *Thunderdome* can be felt right across *Fury Road*.

"Will there be another?" Miller was asked ad infinitum as he peddled his wares before the world. "I honestly don't think so," he replied. "The three feel complete and I don't think we'll come up with anything new enough next time. It's best to leave it as it is for now." Max back in the desert. Alone with his thoughts. But as that old messianic myth has it – after sacrifice comes resurrection.

ABOVE: Aunty Entity gives chase alongside her mechanic Blackfinger (George Spartels) – embracing her part in the *Mad Max* world, Turner would insist on driving her own car.

OPPOSITE: Mel Gibson as the sand-blasted walking myth, Max, who begins and returns to the desert. He would never play the role again.

THE LONG

ROAD

"WE ARE SERVANTS TO THE ZEITGEIST."

– GEORGE MILLER

The Wasteland Weekend was established on a flat expanse of the Mojave Desert, sheltered by a crescent of rocky hills. A match for the compound in *Mad Max 2* thousands of miles away in Broken Hill. Billed as "An Epic Party at the End of the World," thousands come every year, dressed for the occasion: as War Boys and Imperators, Vuvalini and Buzzards, Auntys and Toecutters, Wezs and Ironbars. Max, frankly, has been maxed out. Norma Moriceau's biker-rad designs have become a lifestyle choice. Goggles are de rigueur. Bullet belts haute couture. Cosplay is taken to the level of an unsettling exaltation. The festival of *Mad Max* – unendorsed (who wanted official?) – is a communal experience.

PREVIOUS SPREAD: Dystopian cosplay – capturing the rock'n'roll spirit of the films, devoted fans of *Mad Max* gather in the Mojave Desert for The Wasteland Weekend, a chance to escape their ordinary lives for a post-apocalyptic hellscape.

RIGHT: A Ford Mustang given a *Mad Max* makeover – which brings things symbolically full circle as George Miller had long ago wanted his hero to drive a 1968 Ford Mustang like Steve McQueen in *Bullitt*, but it proved too expensive.

It began in 2004 as Roadwar USA, in which a convoy of replica cars cruised down California's 101 freeway beside an oil tanker. In 2009, they hit the desert. In 2010, George Miller sent a video message, and a sneak peek of something he was preparing in Australia. In 2011, they erected the Wasteland Gates, which led to Wasteland City, including a Wasteland Casino. Pure Bartertown. Guests began to divide into tribes. The Juggers launched into matches of a post-apocalyptic fusion of football and rugby based on the 1989 *Mad Max* rip-off *The Salute of the Jugger*, filmed in Coober Pedy. For almost ten years they displayed the salvaged wreck of the Exxon Valdez from the 1995 *Mad Max* rip-off *Waterworld*. In 2016, the festival proudly boasted of having a working Thunderdome.

"We are servants to the *zeitgeist*," as Miller once said, coming to terms with the fact he would never escape *Mad Max*.

Festivals, museums (Silverton houses the Mad Max 2 Museum sheathed in corrugated iron), race meets, car collections and curated websites proliferated. There were the statutory money-making

BIG FOOT

shifts in media: *Mad Max* books and comics, *Mad Max* video games, *Mad Max* clothing lines. The aesthetic was an MTV mainstay, though Miller dismissed the junkyard fetishising of Duran Duran videos: it was just leather and metal with no organising principle, no poetry.

In any case, it ran deeper than fashion. A *Mad Max* philosophy pervaded culture, a sci-fi punk expressed in bondage gear and throbbing rock, and a mordant fixation with mankind's desolate endgame. Miller would appreciate the connections to the Romantic tradition of the nineteenth century – the pyretic Gothic movement that birthed *Frankenstein*, Jules Verne and the doodad paraphernalia of steampunk. As would Byron Kennedy's mother.

In film, Max's influence was as uncontainable as a wildfire. Miller's world pierced the imaginations of filmmakers. Real cars were thrown around like toys, with the camera in the thick of organised chaos, until CGI made the impossible possible and audiences no longer believed. The exponential stunts of the *Fast and Furious* films owe their excesses to Miller's visual rock 'n' roll. As do the *Bourne* films, the *Mission: Impossibles*, *Ronin*, *Death Proof*, *Baby Driver*, *Drive*. The list goes on.

It wasn't just about style. A delirium of dystopian copycats had followed: *Escape from New York*, *Slipstream*, *Waterworld* (with Dean Semler as cinematographer!), *The Postman*, *Tank Girl*, *Doomsday*, *Pitch Black* (another filmed in Coober Pedy!), *The Book of Eli*, *The Bad Batch*. Before his Oscar-winning *Parasite*, Bong Joon-ho switched the future-shock climate to a new ice age in *Snowpiercer*, set on board an endlessly moving locomotive, populated with a hierarchy of castes. David Michôd's *The Rover*, starring Robert Pattinson and Guy Pearce, is a justly praised Australian thriller in which a hardened loner tracks down the men who stole his car. It is set, a caption announces, "Ten years after the collapse."

Michôd knew there was little point in denying Miller's influence. "From the very first day when Joel and I started talking about the possibility of this movie, we knew we were potentially trespassing on George Miller's property. That is the power of *Mad Max* films."

This tally only skims the barren surface. In 1979, an entire subgenre was born. To be fair, it is as easy to list the brutal futurescapes that preceded *Mad Max*, their parts borrowed and bolted on like Miller's smorgasbord of vehicles: *Metropolis*, *On the Beach*, *The Planet of the Apes*, *The Omega Man*, *Logan's Run*, *Rollerball*. Visceral, terrifying, profound: the *Mad Max* idiom went further, stripping away civilisation to ponder what it means to be human.

"A *MAD MAX* PHILOSOPHY PERVADED CULTURE, A SCI-FI PUNK EXPRESSED IN BONDAGE GEAR AND THROBBING ROCK."

Somewhere in the background, rumours persisted of a fourth *Mad Max* movie. But despite the insistence of the zeitgeist, years passed and nothing.

Their dystopian Australia had offered Miller and Kennedy the world. But they didn't go mad. In the wake of the first film's success, they ventured into television, producing several highly successful series including *The Dismissal* and *Bodyline*, which if anything held to a New Wave sophistication.

After *Mad Max 2*, Miller accepted his first invitation to Hollywood. After all, it had come from Steven Spielberg, who asked him to contribute one of a quartet of stories that made up *Twilight Zone: The Movie*, based on the celebrated Rod Serling-fronted series of weird parables, half-horror, half-sci-fi, and bound to the promise of a discombobulating twist. He was assigned a remake of the famous William Shatner episode from 1963, "Nightmare at 20,000 Feet," about a passenger who sees a terrifying creature out on the wing of his flight and thinks he is going mad. John Lithgow takes over from Shatner. Miller, enjoying all the comforts of a Spielberg production and the familiarity of his own team (Kennedy did sound), had a ball. His is the best of the bunch.

Miller's career tells us strangely little. Rhyme and reason are hard to discern in the mix of success and failure, and the flux of genres. Essentially, *Mad Max Beyond Thunderdome* was his first full Hollywood movie, but on his own terms and in his own backyard.

The baptism by fire was *The Witches of Eastwick* in 1987. All he needed to know about "studio turbulence" was located in this tumultuous adaptation of the John Updike novel about the appearance of the Devil (Jack Nicholson) in the lives of three New England divorcees (Cher, Michelle Pfeiffer, Susan Sarandon). Miller went about things his own way, putting the film first. But in the inverted world of Hollywood not making demands was a sign of weakness. He lost face with producers Peter Guber and Jon Peters, who began to undermine all his requests. "It felt like entering an episode of *The Twilight Zone* rather than shooting one," he said. "Everything was back to front." Nicholson was the one bright spot, allying himself with Miller, advising him to fight fire with fire. Miller refused to shoot a scene unless they met his creative demands. That the film – a gothic comedy taking aim at masculine bravado – holds up is due to Miller's determination. He was learning to survive.

Five years later, *Lorenzo's Oil* was a better experience but a flop. Inspired by Miller's former life as a doctor, it tells the traumatic true story of parents (Susan Sarandon and Nick Nolte) seeking a cure for the brain disease that afflicts their young son. It is delivered without a trace of sentimentality.

The limited output of Miller's transpacific career was not for want of trying.

Planned films ran aground as his mercurial

ABOVE: The bad futures market - in a genre continuum there are those dystopian classics that influenced *Mad Max*, such as *Rollerball* and *Logan's Run* ...

OPPOSITE: ... and there are those dystopian less-than-classics that came in *Mad Max*'s wake, such as ocean-for-desert epic *Waterworld*, with Kevin Costner and Dennis Hopper.

ABOVE: Miller's career seems to veer all over the genre map, but there is an autobiographical vein to his 1992 medical drama, *Lorenzo's Oil*, with Susan Sarandon, Zack O'Malley Greenburg, and Nick Nolte, in tribute to his background as a doctor...

OPPOSITE: ... and even to his 1998 talking-pig sequel, *Babe: Pig in the City*, which is all about the dangers of trying to make it in the big city.

backers lost their nerve. It was exhausting. So much hope and effort would disappear into the air. Two entire years went into a vaunted adaptation of the Carl Sagan novel *Contact*, a Kubrick–Spielberg mix about the theological ramifications of first contact. Do alien radio waves constitute a message from God? Miller was after Jodie Foster or maybe Uma Thurman as the astronomer who deciphers the extra-terrestrial communiqué. But production kept being pushed back as he tinkered with the script, keen to keep things enigmatic, while the studio pressed for explanations. If he bowed to pressure, he said that "it would have let down the source material."

Something had to give, and did. The studio fired him, hiring in his stead Robert Zemeckis, who made a polished sci-fi epic with lead in its boots. Was Miller really naive, as Foster intimated? An extraordinary talent who had no idea how the business worked. He knew enough to sue for breach of contract. And this was Warner Brothers, who had backed so many of his films. As part of the settlement he reclaimed the rights to *Mad Max*.

Max comes to him in dreams. Or what he calls hypnagogic thoughts. Years have passed, and Miller is a different man, a different director. The wild days of his youth are long gone. But from out of the past the damnation of the future called to him. He would recall the moment with absolute clarity.

It is the mid-nineties, and Miller stops at the midpoint of a pedestrian crossing in Los Angeles, the traffic growling, the sunshine unrelenting, an idea taking shape in the form of a challenge. Could he shape a film entirely out of a single chase sequence? A film that was all third act. As quick as light, the creative spark jumping from synapse to synapse, another thought comes to him. A MacGuffin: the precious cargo at the heart of the chase would no longer be petrol but human beings.

Reaching the safety of the other side of the street you like to think he crossed back to where he came from. Yo-yoing like his film, there and back again.

"There was no way I was going to do another *Mad Max* film," he told himself.

It is a few months later, and Miller is around 20,000 feet over the Pacific, like tormented John Lithgow, when the dream returns to him. He wakes from a listless sleep and the fourth *Mad Max* begins to play in his head, not fully formed, but the images are crystal clear: another hellish fleet of rattletrap vehicles against a bright desert sky. A return to the lean simplicity of *Mad Max 2*. Less is so much more.

Max still had Gibson's face at this stage. Inherent in the fabric of what Miller foresaw was the tale of an ageing road warrior heading toward the sunset of his life, like Clint Eastwood's gunslinger in *Unforgiven*. But

caught up in another maelstrom. Miller called it *Fury Road*.

A flashback. To 1995, and Warner Brothers TV, eager for a name property, eager to tame the nihilistic, S&M chic into a toy line, suggested a change of format. *Mad Max* as television show. That intrigued Miller. Giving his post-apocalyptic world the gift of time. Former showrunner on *21 Jump Street* Eric Blakeney was hired. As was the forthright graphic novelist Brendan McCarthy. The comic-book artist saw *Mad Max* as "a sacred artistic duty," insisting it should be a movie. Miller came to realise that a Mad Max television show would have been "very neutered." But ideas lingered, especially McCarthy's vision of Max driving through a storm-wracked landscape with a secret package. Arriving at a vast edifice, ruled over by a tyrant, the package turns out to be a vial of untainted sperm with which he will inseminate a captive teenage girl.

It is 1997, and Miller's creative life is in full spate. *Babe* has become an unexpected smash. Produced by Miller and directed by Chris Noonan, based on the novel by Dick King-Smith, the gentle, moderately effects-driven tale of a talking pig who defies convention to become a sheepherder (rather than bacon), lands $254 million and seven Oscar nominations. It's the photo-negative of *Mad Max*: idyllic, charming, family-orientated. A sequel is inevitably commissioned.

Controversially, Miller slips into the director's chair. *Babe: Pig in the City* has *Thunderdome* tendencies. It expands and intensifies the concept, sending the chirpy pig to sell his fame on the mythical streets of an every-city (a fusion of New York, Sydney and Los Angeles). Was this autobiography? Miller doubles the budget. Baffled by the darker tone, audiences retreated. There are critics who maintain it is a masterpiece.

Concurrently, work continues on *Fury Road*. Miller has put together a brains trust: Blakeney and McCarthy, retained from the scuppered television show; Doug Mitchell, his new producing partner; and costume designer Moriceau (that creative constant). Writing and design work in unison, as Miller comes up with ideas, McCarthy sketches them down.

The bones of Miller's story are clothed in dramatic possibility. The five enslaved wives who are plucked from beneath the nose of cancerous warlord Immortan Joe by his finest warrior – a woman, Furiosa, in search of redemption. She is Aunty Entity unsullied by power. The chase begins: Furiosa and the wives in an armoured rig; Max strapped to the front of one of an armada of hybrid

chariots in hot pursuit, ensnared in another rivalry. They feel it pull away from being a straight *Mad Max* film. He is a passenger in Furiosa's story. Did that matter?

"It couldn't be a male road warrior stealing five wives because that's a different story," said Miller. "Had to be female."

A new angle was emerging. A wildly different take. It was an unconscious thing, maintained Miller, but he was anticipating a near future as much as his far-flung world, a struggle against literally toxic masculinity. This was post-apocalyptic feminism.

Miller is stretched thin, his attention drawn elsewhere: to *Babe 2* and *Happy Feet*, an animated yarn about dancing penguins, all these kids' stories directed by a twin self. He is yin and yang in the same imagination. Tensions grow within the brains trust. McCarthy and Blakeney have differing opinions. Blakeney is jettisoned. In come new recruits: storyboard artists Mark Sexton and Peter Pound enter the eye-shaped nerve centre of Miller's offices in Potts Point, a suburb of Sydney overlooking Elizabeth Bay, to find the room bedecked in outrageous sketches. Things that look impossible.

In 1998, hope. *Variety* runs a story that Universal (the home of *Babe*) will be going into production on a fourth instalment of *Mad Max*, to be released in 2001 or 2002. They suggest that Gibson, now charging $20 million a picture, has not yet been approached.

There is no noticeable urgency within the team of Maxian diviners. At the start of the day, Miller sits in an armchair in the corner of the room, resting his eyelids. The team gathers at the central table waiting on their leader, trying not to disturb his meditative peace. At first, they wonder if he is taking a nap. But not so. Each morning, Miller works through a series of internal calculations, measuring their progress, running the finished movie in his head. Perhaps tapping into that Jungian well from which all stories drank. Then his eyes open. "Okay, I think I'm ready to go now."

Miller was reaching for a state of pure visual stimulus. A thought-wave of sequences like musical notes, flowing from his forehead directly into film form without the intercession of words. "We plotted out the story but basically wrote the screenplay as one extended storyboard, thirty-five hundred panels around a room."

Storyboards were hung upon the walls in twenty-four-frame sequences; after two or three hundred frames it began to play in your head. What could be purer than a script written without words? It was a higher plane of visual rock 'n' roll. There is a 1936 theory of Erwin Panofsky, an art historian and one of the first to take film seriously. Miller surely knows it. How the image short-circuits the reasoning mind to speak directly to the senses.

Try telling that to a studio.

Miller hadn't gone completely mad. There was still dialogue, a discernible three-act structure, and choice characters to be filled with big stars. Names were suggested for a Furiosa opposite

Gibson's Max. Thurman (this was prior to her rampage of revenge in *Kill Bill*), Monica Belluci, Bridget Moynahan. Miller recalled that Charlize Theron's agent had dismissed the idea out of hand. Theron had no idea.

There were doubts even then over Gibson. Was he too old? Too expensive? Would he even do it? Miller's thoughts turned to younger men who might be Max. Brad Pitt was a serious consideration. As was Johnny Depp. McCarthy fought Gibson's corner. This was the opportunity to complete a grand tapestry charting the four ages of Max, the great survivor, from youth to maturity.

It's 2001, and Miller is unaccountably nervous as Gibson peruses the Oval Room, with its charts of stunts foretold, its relentless chase. They haven't worked together since 1985, and Gibson is now an award-winning filmmaker in his own right. That changed the dynamic. "I think George found that quite interesting to figure out," recalled Sexton. Miller fumbles occasionally, backtracking, going over scenes again. Gibson begins to laugh, and Miller knows this to be a good sign. The star is galvanised by everything he sees, the kind of film it might make, but he has a warning for his old friend: "George, it's fucking fantastic and I love it. But we've got to get this going now, because I'm nearly fifty, and I don't even know if I can do it now, let alone in five of six years."

With the failure of the *Babe* sequel, Universal's appetite for *Fury Road* waned. The latent fear re-emerged that Miller was a law unto himself. Doubts were raised over costs. What even was this film? According to Mitchell, "they chickened out." So Miller and Mitchell took it to Fox, where Gibson had a deal. The negotiations took nearly a year. It wasn't clear how these things were going to be pulled off. They arrived at an optimistic budget of $104 million. The plan was to start in May 2003. Down the cast list, among the auditions, Tom Hardy tried out for a War Boy.

"THERE WAS NO WAY I WAS GOING TO DO ANOTHER *MAD MAX* FILM."

– GEORGE MILLER

After much debate, Australia was jettisoned. Gibson demanded to shoot in the USA, which was prohibitively expensive, so a compromise was reached. They relocated to Namibia in Southern Africa, where a dune belt slides up the coast like great folds of yellow sugar, expanding the possibilities of desolation. There were also canyons and flat desert expanses, and the chance to bring good crews over from South Africa. It was ideal, but also a shock. These films were Australian in every sprocket and grain of sand.

It is six weeks from shooting. Production designer Colin Gibson's motley array of mutant vehicles is taking shape in Namibia, but resources are scarce and the budget is soaring. Then realpolitik. In an aftershock from the world-shattering events of 9/11, the Iraq War collapses the American dollar. In a matter of days, thirty per cent of the budget is wiped out. Fox do their sums and pull the plug. Some of the crew have been on the film for four years. With a miserable irony the cars have to be demolished on site. Reduced to a pile of molten steel. They cover over the roads. Miller goes back to his drawing boards, his room of dreams, his *Happy Feet*.

In hindsight, of course, it was a blessing in disguise. "It would have been vastly different,"

OPPOSITE: A bird in the hand – while often derided, the 2006 animated dancing penguin epic *Happy Feet* was such a big hit it gave Miller the collateral to get a fourth *Mad Max* film greenlit.

reflected Mitchell, pondering the *Fury Road* that never was. "Much, much less of a film."

It is 2004, and Miller keeps the fires burning on *Fury Road*. More ideas, more storyboards. All the years of effort have to come to something. And with *Happy Feet* a big hit, and Nicholson's lessons in mind, he only agrees to a sequel if it is a double-deal with *Fury Road*. Warner acquiesce. They are back at the old studio. Full Circle. But the fates have another trial in store for the soft-spoken Odysseus from Chinchilla. A disaster much closer to home.

The story is all too well known. Another legend. How Mel Gibson fell from grace. How Max proved all too mad. There were always odd interviews, strange quotes, a skewed view of the world. Attitudes attributed to his upbringing, especially his father's trenchant Catholic beliefs. Gibson's Oscar-winning achievement as a director with *Braveheart* had been followed by the monumental success of *The Passion of the Christ* and then *Apocalypto*. There is a touch of *Mad Max* in them all: visceral action, crumbling civilisations, messianic urges. And it was no secret that he had enjoyed getting loaded. That went back to his early *Mad Max* days. There was an edge to him. You were never sure what he was thinking. It's one of the things that made him so perfect for the part.

It is 2006, and Gibson is arrested for drunk driving. Hardly unheard of among the A-list, but this is different. During the arrest, he lets forth a torrent of antisemitic bile, as well as sexist innuendo toward a female officer. Hollywood is stupefied. Who was this man? His reputation shattered, Gibson doesn't get another role for four years. Then in 2010, a recording of a toxic row with his then girlfriend, Oksana Grigorieva, is leaked.

"He was completely out of control," recalled Miller. "There was something deeply, profoundly enraged." A *Fury Road* (oh the irony!) with Gibson was an untenable prospect. Miller had no choice but to move on.

It is 2007, and a proposed rendition of the comic-book team-up series *Justice League* becomes another failed Miller epic. Imagine Superman and Batman in the hands of *Mad Max*'s ringmaster. "Like a lot of these things, of course, they're deeply rooted in Greek mythology," he proposes, picturing Hugh Keays-Byrne as Martian Manhunter and Megan Gale (The Valkyrie in *Fury Road*) as Wonder Woman.

It is like a curse. Weeks before production the film is terminated. Various reasons are given. An Australian tax rebate being pulled because the production wasn't Australian enough. Warner Brothers' sudden fears not only over costs (it was looking at a budget of $250 million), but the potential of diluting their superhero brands with too many Batmans and Supermans. Christopher Nolan is preparing a third Batman film, *The Dark Knight Rises*, with another Maxian barrage of action and Hardy as the Humungus-like villain Bane.

And so Miller returned to Max. But this was a new Max, whose world was recalibrated along even more mythic lines. "By the time we got there, not only had Mel hit all the turbulence in his life, but this is not a *Mad Max* in which he's an old warrior. He's meant to be that same contemporary warrior. I guess in the same way that James Bond had been played by various people, it was time to hand over the mantle."

Is this Max the same Max? Only thematically. The wandering hero surviving by his wits. That is his same Interceptor, black on black, but Max is reborn younger, and if anything more tormented. He's even madder, this Max. There is still the ghost of his dead child seared onto his brain like a brand. The spirit of Max is maintained. But Sexton was redrawing storyboards with a younger face.

It is 2009, and there is a green light at the end of the tunnel. *Mad Max: Fury Road* is alive and kicking, and Miller searches for Max, a quest as hard as it was in 1978. How do you reinvent the character without losing the essence of Gibson's antihero? Miller had been convinced about Heath Ledger. The Australian star, pre-Joker, was never officially cast, but he and Miller would meet whenever they were both in Sydney. Ledger shared with Gibson what Miller defined as Max's essential "animal magnetism" (indeed he had actually played Gibson's son in *The Patriot*). It was a paradoxical force; the lure of a caged tiger. "You are drawn to touch," extolled Miller, "but they are untouchable."

Max must be a mystery you never unravel.

But more tragedy, more disruption. Has there ever been a movie that fought so hard *not* to be made? In 2008, Ledger died from an accidental overdose of prescription drugs. So the search went on.

If the rumours are to be believed, Eric Bana, Joel Kinnaman, Jeremy Renner, Michael Fassbender, Eminem (a wild card thing) and Armie Hammer (who had been cast as Miller's Batman and fell foul of his own demons) all tested for Max. But Hardy has something of that doubled-edged charisma. He is both powerfully present and nowhere at all. At one stage, Miller brings Hardy and Hammer in to read together and things get intense. Well, Hardy gets intense, gnashing his teeth and spitting toward his acting partner. He is completely in character. For Miller, it simply feels like this is Max: "I had the same feeling about Tom that I had when Mel Gibson first walked in the room."

It is 2011, in a café somewhere in Los Angeles. After two hours shooting the breeze, one actor to another, the woes of Hollywood, life in general, Hardy gets what he is looking for – Gibson's approval to play Max. "Sure," he says. "It's fine. Knock yourself out. I've got better things to do." Not that Hardy is put at his ease: taking on a role like this, so synonymous with another star, sets you up for failure. There is no grey area, he understands, there will be people who will never accept him as Max. He took that feeling with him into the desert.

"I GUESS IN THE SAME WAY THAT JAMES BOND HAD BEEN PLAYED BY VARIOUS PEOPLE, IT WAS TIME TO HAND OVER THE MANTLE."

– GEORGE MILLER

OPPOSITE: While *Mad Max* lay dormant for decades, Mel Gibson, at first, flourished as a director. Indeed, there was a certain thematic resonance between the civilisation-on-the-brink perils of *Apocalypto* and the car-crazy films of his past.

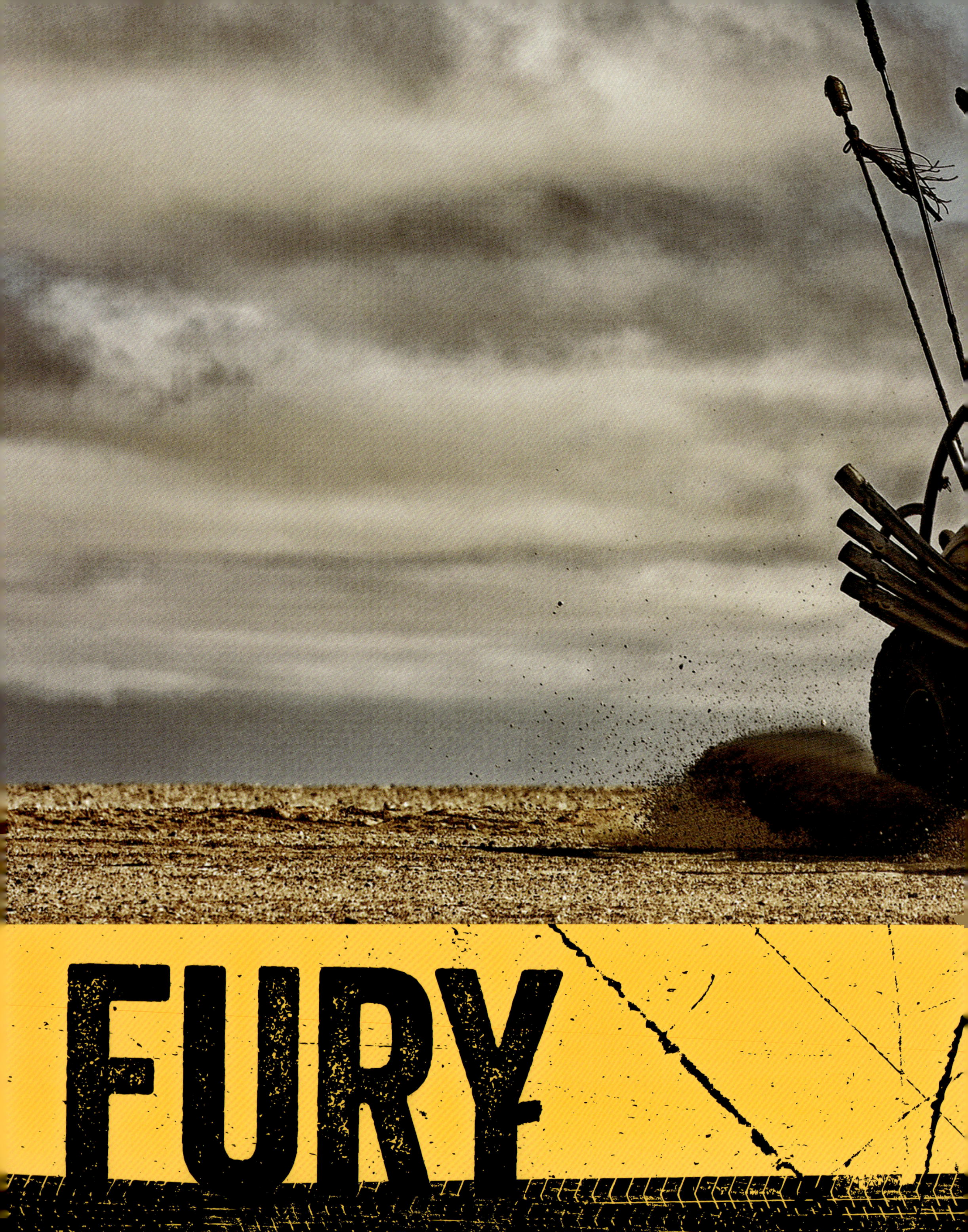
FURY

"I EXIST IN THIS WASTELAND, A MAN REDUCED TO A SINGLE INSTINCT: SURVIVE."

– MAX ROCKATANSKY

The rains lashed Broken Hill, turning sand into pale mud. Flash floods eroded hillsides. Gullies were carved into ancient rocks. Only once in a hundred years did Mother Nature change her mood on this scale. Following the apocalyptic deluge – news reports talked distant cyclones, broiling oceans, climate change – a riot of flowers bloomed out of the desert: blue pincushions, white spoon daisies, pink everlastings. The bleak and bony terrain of *Mad Max 2* resembled *The Wizard of Oz*. The salt lake was home to a flock of pelicans, cooling their happy feet.

PREVIOUS SPREAD: The mad messiah – Max (Tom Hardy) is chained to a cross on the front of Nux's desert-ready Chevrolet Coupe, and to complete the symbolism, supplying blood for the ailing sinner at the wheel. Reference addicts will spot *Mad Max 2*'s Gyro Captain's flight cap, goggles, and skull perched above Max.

OPPOSITE: The heroic Max faces down Immortan Joe's armada of mutant motors. After a troubled production, and complex post, the film became a sensation.

In June 2011, Miller's homecoming had been met with an outburst of fertility. Which was ironic, given his new film was about a scarcity of viable procreation. He felt the old despair rise like a fever. With the budget set, a wary studio finally willing to venture back to the future, Miller had reorientated his production to the scene of *Mad Max 2* – viewed as the *ne plus ultra* of his brutal study in time and motion. *Mad Max: Fury Road* looked set to stall once more. Only now, it was as if Australia itself was rejecting the fourth film.

Warner Brothers suggested holding fire. Wait another year or eighteen months. But there was no guarantee the ecology would return to lifelessness even in that time. And for Miller the urge to start shooting was like craving a drug. Producer Doug Mitchell saw an immediate solution. Go back to Plan A – Namibia. Which was still as rainless as the Gobi. Stick or twist? They twisted. The

studio was largely in the dark as they began shipping cars to another continent.

Then as the new start date loomed, Miller disappeared. He went completely off grid. Only family, friends and close collaborators were informed about the surgery – stents were being inserted into recalcitrant arteries, bolt-on parts for a *Mad Max* heart sturdy enough for what was to come.

As with every *Mad Max* film, if you knew what lay ahead, all the happenstance, the panic, the pain, the big dog wrenching you from your chosen path, you would stick to animated penguins. *Fury Road* became the metaphor of its own making. Like Furiosa's rig, they were driving into an all-consuming sandstorm, dodging lightning bolts, swerving fireballs. An echo, fricasseed in CGI, of the holocaust that sent the world mad.

"I never intended to make a second movie, let alone a fourth," Miller laughed philosophically. "But the story seeds in your head. I've become sort of hardwired for the imaginative life. There's nothing else I can do."

The years of preparation hadn't gone to waste. Alongside the central story existed a vast tapestry of backstories – a landscape of myth and texture through which this linear shockwave of a narrative would fly. Everyone and everything had a backstory. Max and Furiosa, Immortan Joe and his crackpot chorus of addled manhood, the untarnished Wives, the Citadel, the armada of deviant vehicles, even their steering wheels had become character totems, personalised with Day of the Dead skulls.

Take for instance The Doof Warrior (in fact, part-Maori, part-English, part-Australian singer-songwriter iOTA, or Sean Hape), the blind guitarist who serenades the War Boys with thrash metal chords like an army bugler, backed by a thunderous chorus of taiko drums. The note passed to agents described the character inconclusively as a "mix of Keith Richards and a scarecrow." According to the director, he is wearing the face of his dead mother. Blind since birth, this musical prodigy was found in the desert by Immortan Joe, carrying his mother's severed head. The scarlet long johns amp up The Gyro Captain's

jester aesthetic with a touch of Angus Young from AC/DC. And he is attached to a bungee-like harness like a marionette or a Thunderdome contestant.

His twin-necked axe was built out of a hospital bedpan and delivered great plumes of flame like a burning oil well. The first version was a prop. Then Miller visited the workshop, smiled his beatific smile, and said that he couldn't wait to hear it play. So they made it playable. On set.

"I just sort of got up there and jammed," reported iOTA. "Whatever I could come up with. It's a double-neck guitar, so it's a bass and six-string electric."

Riffs from AC/DC, Zeppelin and Soundgarden congeal into a snarling battle cry, urging the War Boys on. A "doof" is Aussie slang for an outdoor rave music event, from the drumbeat: *"doof, doof, doof."*

He was the living emblem of *Fury Road*. Visual rock 'n' roll.

Remarkably, there were ideas deemed too mad. Even for Miller. John Howard's The People Eater, a leprous and corpulent former banker allied to Immortan Joe, was originally going to walk around with a continuous erection. This was part of their process. The writers would go too far and Miller would rein them in. But the excess still seethed beneath the surface.

As the delays lengthened into years, there was time to write novellas and additional scripts, and storyboard an entire graphic novel. These included the story of Furiosa: how she became shackled to Joe's turbo-charged cult as a child; how she lost her left arm, and stoked her pain and resentment like a boiler. Charlize Theron got to read it, to understand what lay below the surface. A backstory that has become a prequel. And they included another adventure for Max in the endless desert. Named *The Wasteland*, it still hovers on

ABOVE: George Miller frames a shot from inside the cab of the War Rig, with director of photography John Seale, who though well into his seventies could be found hanging off vehicles, his head inches from the ground, operating the camera.

OPPOSITE: Charge of the headlight brigade - The Doof Warrior (played by singer-songwriter iOTA) was Miller's idea of what a military bugler might look like in his warped future. With an entire backstory written for the character, there is every chance he will be reborn in the prequel *Furiosa*.

Miller's to-do list, if he can summon the energy and the courage to return to the future for a sixth time.

It wasn't just the macrocosm of the world that grew; Miller added layer upon layer to the engine of *Fury Road*, the central chase, reinventing action cinema. Angles, colours, shots, stunts, sequences, an intricate marriage of character and forward momentum. This was to be a deranged yet precision planned adventure where detail was God: Madder Max.

Nico Lathouris was enrolled into the brains trust. He was his own myth, having played a nervy mechanic in *Mad Max* before turning to screenwriting. Miller-like, he viewed the work in symbolic terms. How the film could be divided into three chases that take Max and Furiosa from confrontation to obligation to devotion. "I tried to figure out the psychology of it," he said. The toxic storm was a manifestation of Max's mind.

The plot remained whimsically straightforward, yet almost dizzyingly allusive. Miller compressed his entire dystopian freak zone into three days, structured as a ricochet in which Furiosa and Max attempt to ferry the Wives to the freedom of the Green Place in a turbo-charged tanker called the War Rig, discover it's long gone, and make for the very place they started – the Citadel. In the process, ridding the world of Immortan Joe and his rabid War Boys. There and back again. A plot tied to a bungee cord.

All of it was informed by, yet not beholden to, the films that had come before. With Gibson gone, Miller began to enjoy the looseness this afforded the franchise, as if *Mad Max* were a style, a mood or a collection of raggedy fairy tales, rather than a stiff cinematic universe drawn tight with narrative threads. It's a mythological connection, he insisted, stories reshaping themselves in the desert heat.

Hints of films past dance through *Fury Road* like dust devils. Zoë Kravitz's Toast the Knowing playing the same miniature hurdy-gurdy that enchanted The Feral Kid in *Mad Max 2*. The Gyro Captain's skull, complete with pilot's cap and goggles, leers over Max when he's strapped to the front of Nux's supercharged 1935 Chevrolet Coupé. Human hood ornaments go back to *Mad Max 2*. As does the cartridge fizzling in Max's sawn-off shotgun. And one of Immortan Joe's guards sporting a boomerang as a weapon. There are references to references: the Buzzards' spiky cars are a tribute to the spiky VW Beetle in Peter Weir's *The Cars That Ate Paris*. The list goes on, all these Maxian stepping stones. The Wives' quarters have the geodesic frame of a Thunderdome. Rictus Erectus looks like Lord Humungus. Furiosa's eye swollen shut in the final flurry is a match for Max's lopsided face at the end of *Mad Max 2*.

The search for Furiosa, alongside a younger Max, always led Miller back to the same place. They discussed names – Uma Thurman, Megan Gale – but he couldn't think of anyone but Theron. Beneath the beauty there was something unbreakable, even intimidating.

She had a former dancer's discipline and a dramatic backstory. Theron grew up on a farm in Benoni, South Africa, a tyrannical upbringing brought to a close when she witnessed her mother shoot her alcoholic father in self-defence. There were currents in *Fury Road* that ran deep for the leading lady. Following a

OPPOSITE TOP: Four of the precious Five Wives – from left: Capable (Riley Keough), The Dag (Abbey Lee), Cheedo the Fragile (Courtney Eaton), and Toast the Knowing (Zoe Kravitz) ...

OPPOSITE: ... According to Kravitz, Miller had asked potential actresses to tell him a story at the audition, and then to read from an unrelated script. It was those who expressed a unique sensibility that won the part.

TOP: Nux's super-charged Chevrolet and a Plymouth Rock given a porcupine upgrade. The spikes were a tribute to the influence of Peter Weir's *The Cars That Ate Paris,* and its spiky automobiles, had on the original *Mad Max*.

ABOVE: Tom Hardy reinvents Max – a blood bank for the War Boys, the idea was for Max to start the film as much property as the Five Wives. The shotgun is a tribute to the one Mel Gibson brandishes in *Mad Max 2*.

training in ballet, she had risen to the occasion in Hollywood: *The Devil's Advocate*, *Mighty Joe Young*, *North Country*, and winning an Oscar, her looks smothered, as female serial killer Aileen Wuornos in *Monster*. She had courage as a performer.

As soon as she spoke to Miller she knew. "He was so excited about creating an antiheroic woman . . . Driven by pure human flaws."

Those names are repurposed objects as much as the cars. With Furiosa, Miller simply wanted that anger. Her designation, Imperator, was an old Roman term. This is a future reawakening ancient codes: Roman, Nordic, Aztec.

One of the many triumphs of *Fury Road* is how easily the film is shared between Max and Furiosa. She takes shape in an instant: those green eyes beacons of wrath, her body taut as a bowstring, maybe not all of it a matter of acting. For Miller it was an exalting thing to watch his character come to life: "She arose out of the architecture of the story."

"HE WAS SO EXCITED ABOUT CREATING AN ANTIHEROIC WOMAN ... DRIVEN BY PURE HUMAN FLAWS."

– CHARLIZE THERON

It is 3am when she calls Miller. They are days from shooting. There's no preamble, she is Furiosa already: "I want to shave my hair." She isn't asking. He takes a breath, visualising the idea, feeling it, knowing she's right. "Yes," he says eagerly. Theron wants to get real. Furiosa wouldn't bother with hair in the heat and the dust and the anger. The nerve centre of the film, the mesmerising Imperator stands in vivid contrast to the angelic Wives in muslin sashes and bespoke chastity belts. Basically, she looks like Max.

ABOVE: Miller attempts to communicate his vision to a long-suffering Charlize Theron as Furiosa. The actress valiantly upheld her side of the deal through a long and often baffling shoot in Namibia.

OPPOSITE: Something of her frustration found an outlet in her performance. Miller could see how she arose out of the story to be the film's anchoring presence.

TOP: Theron and Miller discuss shotgun etiquette – Furiosa's prosthetic arm was created with a mix of practical and digital effects, with Miller determined only to use CGI if all other avenues had been exhausted.

ABOVE: Method in their madness – Furiosa's violent introduction to Max may have channelled a fair amount of the actors' mutual dislike.

For *Fury Road*, the archetype was essentially split in two: male and female, Max and Furiosa. Two parts of one idea. So the severed arm is not for show. There are no gimmicks in the desert of the future. Logic fuels design. Function accentuates theme. This was to mirror Max. As he had his leg in a brace (never quite seen in *Fury Road*), so she has lost an arm. There were no Swiss Army blades or a concealed crossbow. It was based in part on the bitterly comical image of a Rwandan man who had replaced a severed arm with a strap-on cigarette holder. The design team incorporated an old pair of dental pliers into the make-do mechanics of the wearable prosthetic, to be enhanced with CGI in post. "Bad-ass," grinned Theron when it finally took shape.

Parallels abound. She's hardly a talker, but she can handle a rig. Both Max and Furiosa have sawn-off shotguns. And it's Max's blood that keeps her alive at the end. Theron had her breasts strapped down; bandaging became a motif – Furiosa and her old wounds. The costume was about protection. Survival. The engine oil she smears across her eyes, said hair and make-up designer Lesley Vanderwalt, "was like she was putting on her war paint."

Furiosa isn't saving anyone. She is taking

the thing that matters most to Joe – these Wives. She never even calls them by their names. It is pure revenge. Then the Wives are hardly victims, but a gaggle of amusingly grouchy young women determined not to be breeding stock.

When it came to casting, Miller still had madness in his methods. Tell me a story, he asked prospective Wives. One about either the happiest or saddest thing that has ever happened to you. How far they went, how open they were with him, told him everything.

By the second round they were workshopping scenes from unrelated scripts: *When Harry Met Sally*, say, or *Erin Brockovich*. Do with it what you will, instructed Miller. The winners caught on to his sense of adventure: Rosie Huntington-Whitely (Angharad the Splendid, the pregnant favourite), Kravitz (Toast the Knowing), Riley Keough (Capable), and Courtney Eaton (Cheedo the Fragile). Did it say something that two of them were descended from rock stars? For The Dag, Abbey Lee did a full rendition of Peter Finch's meltdown from *Network* as a Southern Pentecostal preacher. This glow of youth is given a counterpoint in the Vuvalini, the gaggle of matriarchal biker chicks, faces like parchment, who join the fray for the final act.

Cut to the chase.

From 2 June 2012, for six long, hot, hateful months they shot in Namibia. Oldest desert

ABOVE: Oncoming traffic - Capable, Cheedo the Fragile, and The Splendid Angharad (Rosie Huntington-Whitely) take a salutary look back at their pursuers. Miller was determined his new film was centred on a female experience.

on the planet say geologists. The notorious Skeleton Coast is named for the vessels left to rot on the rocks like the ribs of leviathans. There was a vibe, for sure. The local Bushmen christened it "The Land God Made in Anger."

"Out here everything hurts," snaps Furiosa, when The Splendid Angharad winces at the graze left by a passing bullet. Welcome to the film.

East of their base at Swakopmund was the Moon Landscape, rocky and undulating in the style of Broken Hill or Coober Pedy. Here they shot Furiosa's War Rig assailed by the Buzzards, an extraordinary volley of action featuring buzzsaws on extendable arms. A crescendo to any mortal film, here it's mere overture. Per the mythos: The Buzzards live in the Sunken City (a cavernous network the size of an airport), babble in Russian, drive the Weir-esque porcupine cars (including a Plymouth Sedan in honour of *Duel*), and are the lowest of the low.

"For each of the stunts, we had looked at what anybody else had ever done before and figured out how to up the ante," said stunt co-ordinator Guy Norris, who had broken a leg on *Mad Max 2*. Including what *they* had done before.

Production designer Colin Gibson had been on the *Fury Road* for years. He had melted an entire convoy in 2001. For the second iteration of vehicles, Miller wanted to be surprised. Gibson's instinct was to return to the "once-we-were-kings" elegance of old models, only melded into brutish combinations like some form of radioactive mutation. Joe's kingly ride is a

RIGHT: Arguably, the most enduring visual idea out of a feast of visual invention, the glorious polecats were inspired by a mix of Cirque du Soleil acrobatics and the founding father of the *Mad Max* aesthetic, Buster Keaton, swinging on a drainpipe before they even had sound.

"WE HAD LOOKED AT WHAT ANYBODY ELSE HAD EVER DONE BEFORE AND FIGURED OUT HOW TO UP THE ANTE."

– GUY NORRIS

1959 Cadillac Coupe de Ville built atop a 1959 Cadillac Coupe de Ville; the Peacemaker, commanded by The Bullet Farmer (Richard Carter), is a tracked Ripsaw EV1 with a Valiant Charger body, which snorted through the desert thanks to a V8 engine.

The design team were driven by the concept of salvage. But with a view to both battle and beauty. The punk-art retrofitting of *Mad Max 2* was taken to a nonpareil rapture. It was only in "the fetish," said Gibson, that the world was defined. "It's only in that odd flash that we have to a chance to say something about the end of the world. We try to imply it's not just a bunch of brutal yahoos in love with V8s, but also a huge well of guilt about everything that had been lost."

Underneath the armour-plating of the War Rig was a Czech eighteen-wheel Tatra-T815. The cab was customised, including the rear end of a Chevrolet Fleetmaster. Three were made in total and a separate cab for interiors. "It's the old technology that survived," said Miller.

The War Rig is the film's anchoring image: tanker, battleship, getaway vehicle, Moby Dick of the dark desert highway; brute expression of encrusted manhood driven by an enraged woman.

As with any artistic medium, said Miller, the poetics of film are open to interpretation. People decide what a film means to them. Often it's geographical. In South Africa, *Babe* was taken as a parable about apartheid. The undercurrent is all important. Nevertheless, he insisted, there is design. "You must have very

clear dramaturgical strategies to find your path through. There is a craft to it."

Fury Road went back to those Campbellian basics, but with greater purpose than ever. Stories, said Miller, were "how we make sense of the world." As well as projecting a grim future, the net result of mankind's madness, *Fury Road* was also unpicking the present.

It had been there all along – the desert as a palimpsest of the now. And Miller was using the tenets of action and disaster moves, science-fiction, even war movies, to tune into a feminist angle. Enter Eve Ensler, author

of *The Vagina Monologues*. He had heard her on Australian radio, enthralled by what she said, and invited her to join the production in Namibia to head up a workshop, principally with the Five Wives. Ahead of time, he sent over audio files containing his extensive thoughts on the film's plot, themes and characters. What he called his "tellings."

For a week, Ensler spoke on the oppression of women in war zones, places such as Bosnia, Kosovo, Afghanistan, and the Congo. As well as sex trafficking in America. What was it like to be a sex slave? What were the broader political implications? To give, she said, "a perspective on violence against women around the world." The influence ran both ways; Miller was using the dystopia of the here and now to inform the oppression of the future: "You have to prepare the world," he explained. Ensler's audiences grew in size, as even the stuntmen came by to listen. She remained a huge proponent of the film: "One of the great things about this film is that when you have women on your side, you have a better chance of surviving."

Which stands in contrast to the furies coursing between Theron and Hardy.

ABOVE: Immortan Joe (Hugh Keays-Byrne) on the bridge of his custom-built flagship – The Gigahorse embodied the new design aesthetic of classic-model mash-ups, with two Cadillac Coupe de Villes stacked on top of each other.

OPPOSITE: Yet another take on the *Fury Road* – editor Margaret Sixel would eventually have to discover a film from over 480 hours of footage, or twenty days-worth of takes.

OPPOSITE: Hardy, an unfamiliar face in familiar leathers – the question of who could replace Mel Gibson in his signature role came down to a feeling for George Miller. And Hardy evoked the same elusive, animal charisma he had seen in Gibson.

BELOW: Round the Benz – but like Theron, Hardy struggled to fathom what it was Miller had in mind, becoming increasingly frustrated (and difficult) with the shoot.

Hardy was six weeks old when they shot the original *Mad Max*. And he had his backstory. The London-born son of an artist and novelist, he came up through modelling to fulfil his dream of emulating Gary Oldman with a varied and provocative acting career: *Band of Brothers*, *Black Hawk Down*, *Inception*, *Bronson*, *Locke*. But behavioural problems as a child led to dark periods of drug addiction as a young man. Rumours persisted that he was unpredictable on set.

He dismissed them as myths. "But do I go to places which are scary and uncomfortable for some people? Yes."

After they met, Mel Gibson had called Hardy's agent. "I think you've found someone who is crazier than I am."

Hardy came to the film naive about what Max was about to ask of him. Not necessarily physically, but in terms of the Miller method. Both Hardy and Theron struggled to grasp the bigger picture. Entire days could be dedicated to seconds of screentime. A glance, a grimace, a foot pressed to the metal. Miller had the pictures in his head, said Hardy, "and the actors were a bunch of investigators." Miller hadn't directed human beings for a decade. All these questions were like flies buzzing around his head.

What's more, Hardy was a Method guy. He lived his roles. And right now he was channelling a desolate personality barely able to speak (Max has sixty-three lines in total, Furiosa eighty). There were rumours of an adventurous early cut in which Max didn't speak at all. Pure Buster Keaton. Trying to plumb Max's depths, the actor would shut himself off. That edge cut both ways.

Even in the 2001 Gibson version of *Fury Road* there had been an increase in Max's madness. "Mel's character was going to be completely insane," recalled Mark Sexton. A gibbering, blathering, ranting wreck.

Hardy would thaw out as Max warmed up. Things got easier. "The story is all about self-preservation," reflected Miller, once the dust had settled. "If it's an advantage to you to kill another character, then you should do it and you don't think twice about it. I think that crept into the actors."

Theron made no bones about it. "We fucking went at it, yeah. And on other days he and George went at it."

Anger can have its benefits. This is *Mad Max*. She is Furiosa. Their first violent confrontation was filmed at Blanky Flats to the north, where the clouds of dust billowed up behind Immortan Joe's shimmering armada like a demonic twist on the "mirage" from *Lawrence of Arabia*. The War Rig has stalled after the storm, and Max emerges from a premature burial, encased in a steel mask and manacled to an unconscious Nux. All Furiosa sees is pure threat. What is the opposite of meet cute? Bond ugly.

"DO I GO TO PLACES WHICH ARE SCARY AND UNCOMFORTABLE FOR SOME PEOPLE? YES."

– TOM HARDY

BELOW: Survival of the maddest – in the final confrontation, designed like a dance number, Max is constantly attempting to get back to Furiosa.

Well, Miller had a dream. On the morning they were due to begin the sequence, he explained to fight co-ordinator Greg Van Borssum that the ensuing combat was to be a love scene.

"*What the fuck*," mouthed Theron.

A raging set-to using everything that comes to hand – bolt-cutters, car door, hose pipes: heavy duty props – becomes a mirror of the power struggle within the film and within the production. It is wordlessly choreographed to the edge of slapstick. But brutal. No quarter is given to gender. Finally, a sense of understanding emerges. That they are alike. And they want to survive. Between takes they wouldn't even look at each other.

How do you define Max's relationship with Furiosa? It is the heartbeat of the film. According to history, Max is essentially a loner, jarred into heroism by human contact. That is no different here, but there is something more, something deeper. Is it love? Respect? What? Max and Furiosa, these lost souls, are meant for one another.

Pondering the idea of romance while promoting the third film (the studio had expressed disappointment that Max and Aunty Entity never got it on in Bartertown), Miller declared Max's to be a monastic existence. "Max certainly doesn't want love, because it's an impediment – it's not conducive to survival to be emotionally involved with somebody else,

TOP: Miller and Max – a rare moment of calm between director Miller and star Hardy. There is an argument that Hardy, who comes at a role from within, was channelling the state-of-mind of his character.

ABOVE: There and back again – Max proposes they turn the War Rig around and go back the way they came. Which is exactly what he does in *Mad Max 2* and *Thunderdome*, finishing the film by heading into oncoming traffic.

RIGHT: Nicholas Hoult, as the turncoat War Boy Nux, was there to inject some innocence and humour into the chaos. He was also a symbol of how young men fall under the spell of demagogues.

because you've got two people to worry about. As for sex . . . we never figured it out."

For all the S&M accoutrements, sex has remained at the margins of these films. The action possesses its own erotic ecstasy. *Fury Road* surges to a series of ever-increasing climaxes. The only bodily fluids Max and Furiosa share is a battlefield blood transfusion. It's the most romantic scene in the series.

After Toecutter's crew, Humungus's marauders and Aunty's rabble, *Fury Road* gives us the War Boys.

Nicholas Hoult's Nux is our chief guide to the screwball conventions of the new gang, an enthusiastically hellbent driver, suffering from a vague but prevalent form of radioactive debilitation. In a fetching detail, the twin tumours bulging from his clavicle have been tattooed with smiley faces. Hoult drew them himself. Larry and Barry. He is effectively a child, an innocent. Hoult had made the transition from child stardom in *About a Boy* to *A Single Man*, *Clash of the Titans*, the *X-Men* films. He still looks so young.

Subdivided into Drivers, Spikers and Polecats, the War Boys are a death cult who look like death. Vanderwalt made them as bald and pale as corpses, adding cancerous lesions, and contours to accentuate their skulls. They are living a half-life. *Fury Road* is the first of the *Mad Max* films to conjecture a consequence of radioactive fallout. Purity is now a theme. Loaded up with Immortan Joe's deranged cant, they are cannon fodder in a despot's wild urges. Nux is delighted to perish: "If I am going to die, I'm going to die historic, on the fury road!"

Miller was making explicit the feedback loop of his mythology. Where once Max had

been perceived in the Viking tradition, now these death-or-glory berserkers are transfixed by the promise of a petrolheaded Valhalla awaiting them in the afterlife. It's another warped religion.

When it came to Immortan Joe, a fixed and despicable figure amid the shifting banks of story, Miller had been thinking about how effective Hugh Keays-Byrne had been in *Mad Max*. The actor had virtually invented his gang of bikers, a cult leader on- and offscreen, his personality bursting through the binds of character. Miller wanted that authority again. And he realised that was the answer. In another doubling of actor in a different part, he called Keays-Byrne and asked if he might be interested. His old friend took a breath and said, "Okay."

All these years later, their means millions of dollars more elaborate, Keays-Byrne became Immortan Joe, worshipped by his tribe of stunties, War Boys to their beating hearts, and most of the crew. His costume fitted, his long, white hair quivering in the breeze (like Aunty's ravishing locks, and an inversion of Furiosa – a notable realignment of gender tropes in the irradiated future), he would stride out of his trailer and bellow "Daddy's here," silencing the set. Like Hardy he went deep into character. But he was more playful underneath, insisted Miller, paying tribute to Keays-Byrne, who died in December 2020, making *Fury Road* his last great ride. In the moment, however, he could be very scary.

"He did so much of my work for me," laughed Abbey Lee, who one afternoon began hyperventilating in his presence. They had to stop filming for her to breathe into a paper bag.

ABOVE: Poisoned by a radioactive hangover, the War Boys were designed to resemble Mexican Day of the Dead masks with shaved heads, pale skin, and smudged eyes. They live a half-life.

OPPOSITE: Miller orchestrates a fitting death for Immortan Joe – to have his jaw ripped off by chain reaction, his mask literally entangled in a chain, which becomes entangled with a wheel. His foul voice is finally silenced.

BELOW: Leader of the pack – bringing back *Mad Max*'s Keays-Byrne was another example of the mythological connective tissue with the old films. It is a world where stories are constantly recycled.

Immortan Joe is a demagogue, a self-appointed godhead to a car cult, giving a very literal definition to the term "autocratic." Like his skinny minions, he began as bald as a coot, only smeared in blue paint, a joke perhaps at the expense of *Braveheart*. But when it came to it there were too many blue dudes populating recent cinema. So they made him white: a plasterboard face concealed beneath an oxygen mask, a bladder heaving on his shoulders, his back a landscape of tumours. Another tableau of the after-effects of radiation. In his lust for more healthy heirs – he has two blood sons thus far: the robust but dim-witted hulk Rictus Erectus (Nathan Jones) and the smart but diminutive Corpus Colossus (Quentin Kenihan, born with brittle bone disease) – and with a clutch of obstreperous wives, he is Henry VIII reborn. Keays-Byrne took a wider view. Immortan Joe is doing his bit to rebuild society.

"So he sees himself very much as a renaissance man," he smiled.

His sugar-loaf Citadel (for Miller, a historical constant, the great edifice from which the few dominate the many) was captured at Cape Town Film Studios and back at Fox Studios in Sydney during the reshoots, then extended with the first smears of CGI ever put to the Maxian world. There was more CGI used than is apparent: erasing rigging, shifting backgrounds, saving lives.

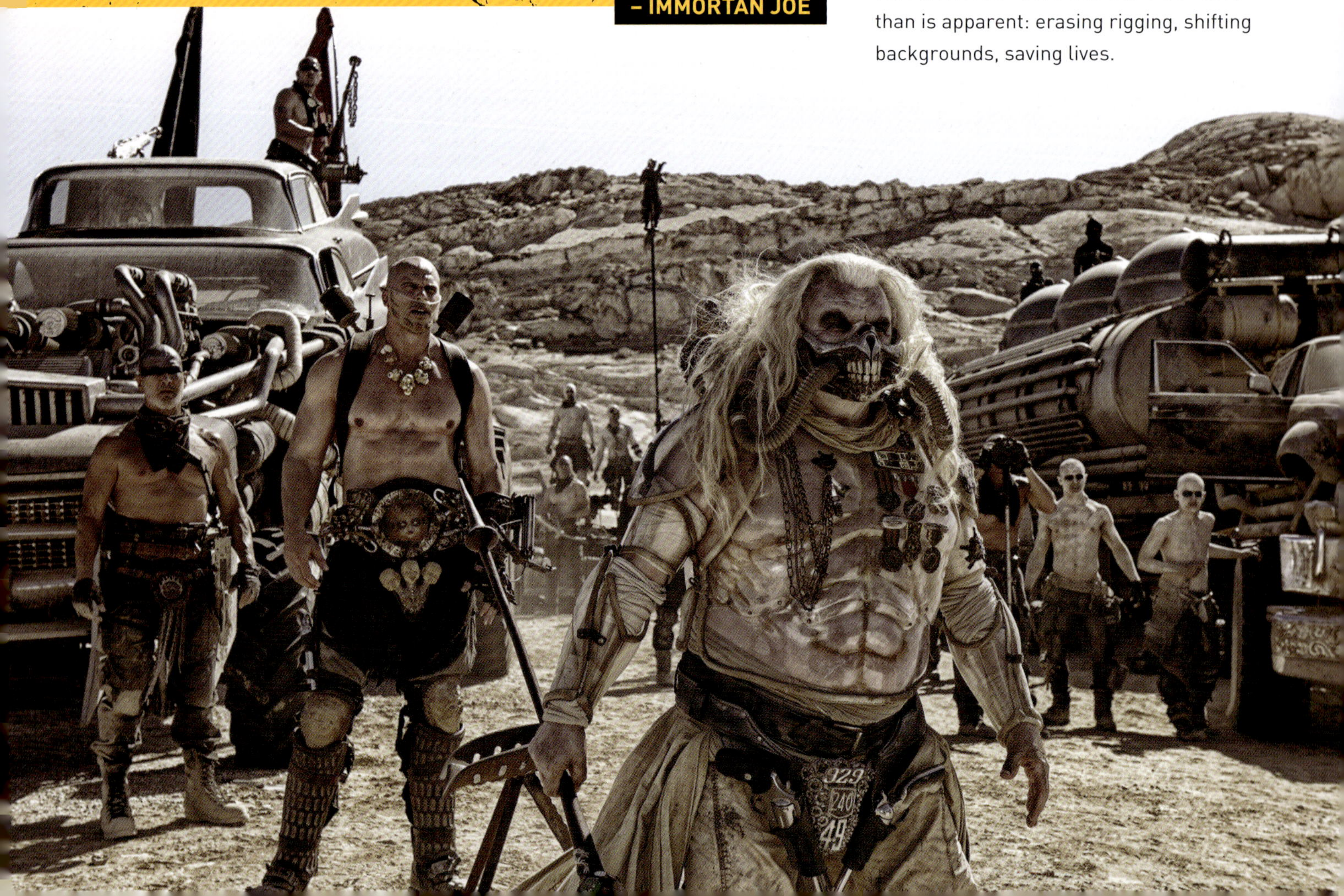

Was there ever any sense they were making the greatest action movie of all time? There was such frustration, and so many tears. What emerged was the apotheosis of Miller's long-held beliefs. "One can look at a different part of the frame each time one watches *Fury Road* and see an entirely different film," raved Chuck Bowen in *Slant*.

The deal gone bad with the Rock Riders – guzzaline for safe passage – was filmed between orange crags in the Swakop River Valley. The Rock Riders are a biker gang (in homage to Toecutter's crew) pimped as Rastafarians in ski goggles. They brought in the best trick riders in the world: it was a case of negotiating razor-edged trails like angry mountain goats, launching themselves diagonally over the tanker, throwing a smoke bomb, so riding one-handed, then landing. Five of them, all at once. Repeatedly. Stephen Gall (five times Australian Motocross champion) pulled off the somersault. Then Miller put a camera on the back of his bike for a rider's perspective, as he had done long ago on *Mad Max*. The added weight almost dragged Gall under the bike.

Safety was still an issue. How do you keep the lid on a film where every day is a big stunt day? Yet Miller's anxiety was as rich a resource as the Aqua-Cola (water) drawn up through the rocks of the Citadel. The film is wired to an adrenalised terror. Every moment is shot through with panic.

Technically, they were in a realm beyond even the fantasies of the young men holding on for dear life on *Mad Max*. Seventy-year-old John Seale came out of retirement to replace Dean Semler as cinematographer, with a magician's chest at his disposal, including over sixty digital cameras. Chief among his wonders was a roof-mounted, gyro-stabilised crane grasping a 360-degree rotating camera – known to the camera boys as the "Edge Arm" – which could reach into a scene. Miller didn't want the viewer to observe the carnage, he wanted to dangle them among the collisions like bait on a fishing line.

"As you accumulate some degree of craft and work with people that you worked with before, you can get pretty close to what you set out to do," he observed.

For all the gizmos and facilities $150 million affords you, Miller had come to realise that, in the end, it is intuition that calls the shots. The intellectual stuff, the strategising, all the

storyboarding, are just, he said, "fuelling the engine." In the heat of the moment (which extended for six months) you go with the gut. *Mad Max* must never be mechanical.

Nevertheless, he could watch an instantaneous high-definition feed – known to all as "Fury TV"– tallying those atomic moments that would combine into the storyboards that flowed across his walls. "Cinema is a mosaic art," he said. That instinctive back and forth between the telling detail and the wider view. The audience knowing where they were at any moment.

They moved across Namibia, bulldozing strips of land into the vestiges of roads. *Fury Road* has very little in the way of tarmac. They follow trails, negotiate barren flats, grind through mud. The former Green Place proves to be a quagmire, a ruined pocket of earth (these are stark environmental warnings for the contemporary world) filmed on salt pans called the Paaltjies. The War Rig's struggles (it gasps like a beast) in a veil of digitally enhanced cobalt-blue nightfall. This is the

ABOVE: Slit (Josh Helman) targets his quarry – before each day's shoot, The War Boys actors and stuntmen would gather to chant, getting themselves in the mood. Helman likened the whole production to opera, you have permission to be over the top.

RIGHT: Miller wanted an explosion like no other – rather than one simple boom, his team triggered another chain-reaction, with a series of detonations that danced up a remote-controlled tanker filled with over 1,000 litres of fuel.

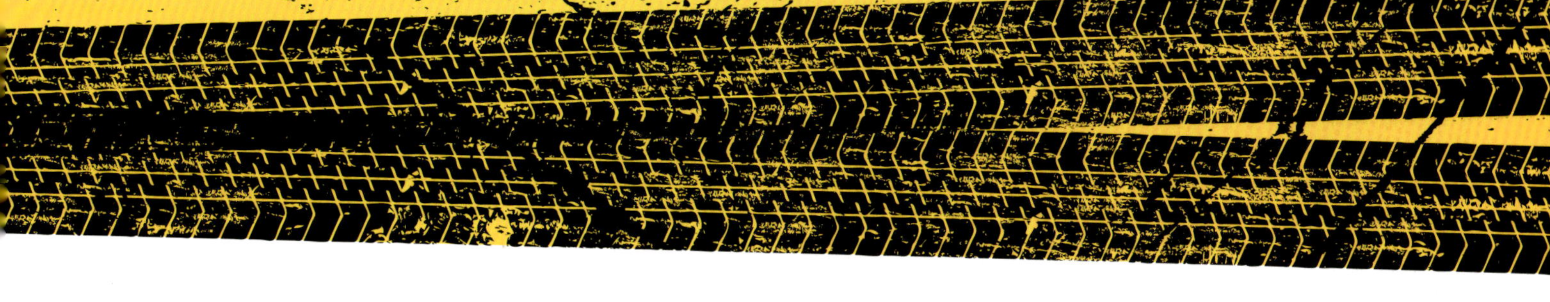

glow of a poisoned world. The Neverland of old dreams. But such colour is a new energy. Communication flares explode in cloudbursts of red or yellow powder, and the War Boys spray paint their demented grins in silver (an edible mist used in cake decorating).

There are sights in *Fury Road* that feel stronger than our own memories. Images etched into our psyches. The Polecats swaying to the film's signature movement – back and forth. Lethal acrobats. Newtonian physics their plaything. The Edge Arm following every swoop. Inspiration came to Miller from a combination of Cirque du Soleil, Keaton dangling from a drainpipe in *Three Ages*, Toecutter's boys pole vaulting onto a tanker in *Mad Max*, and that gut feeling for the majestic potential of cinema. He accepted it must be CGI. But Norris made it real. "A lot of effort went into training guys in Chinese pole work. Then a friend of mine who had worked for Cirque du Soleil took it a step further, heading up an eight-week training program."

After they figured out the perfect pivot point with the counterweight, like a desk toy, they were swinging stuntmen to their heart's content. When Miller saw the test footage he wept. Byron Kennedy would have loved this.

The Polecats take a starring role as the film rebounds back to the Citadel through the ranks of incensed War Boys. In what Norris called "the dancing truck sequence." Like a dance number from a forties musical, Max and Furiosa must be kept apart for as long as possible: she is at the wheel and he is tapdancing from vehicle to vehicle, trying to get back to her. Norris and his team kept asking themselves, how do we interrupt that process and have another set piece? Everything was about escalation.

Finally, the rig must roll. Nux sacrificing himself to bring down a sandstone arch upon what's left of Joe's band. Miller banished any thought of doing it with CGI. After so much toil in the desert that would be a betrayal of their core beliefs. There had to be a foolhardy human at the wheel. Full circle. That was Lee Adamson, wrapped, as Dennis Williams once was, in a roll cage. Naturally, Miller was going to take it further than the crash landing of *Mad Max 2*.

"The whole point was to do it down the barrel."

These are Miller's instructions. The truck has to flip and land precisely between two rocks, coming to a halt a few feet in front of the camera. This isn't Namibian soil – fittingly, it is the red Australian soil of Penrith, Sydney, a year after principal photography. The truck is equipped with a nitrogen gas cannon to push it off its wheels. Adamson has done test runs. A preliminary burst of nitro was enough to send him jack-knifing toward catering. On the day, as Adamson is strapped in, Miller feels the old nerves behind his bank of screens, each capturing the view of eight cameras. On cue, Adamson wrenches the wheel and fires the cannon. The rig spins in the air, then grinds into the earth, nothing but dust, before sliding to its mark on the very first take. Miller panics, certain he has seen the driver's head strike the roof of the cab. The crew race to the felled rig. Dust clears. The door is prised open, and Adamson emerges to thunderous applause. Full circle.

What Miller had seen was the dummy of Nux bouncing in the cab.

"All this is such fun," declared Anthony Lane in *The New*

Yorker, "and it teeters so close to insanity, with a hundred-and-fifty vehicles at Miller's disposal, and with a pack of cameras sent into the fracas like baying hounds on a scent, that you come out asking, Why is this movie not an unholy mess?"

The answer to that question is Margaret Sixel. Miller was adamant his wife edit the film, precisely because she had never done action before. And because she wasn't a man. This was *Fury Road* philosophy: male thinking would slide back into the old ways; a female perspective would open up new possibilities. Over her shoulder, Miller would lower the frame rate until a grace was attained, then let it spring back to twenty-four frames as if time was elastic.

Over eighteen months Sixel toiled to make sense of 470 hours of footage (it took three months to watch it). Versions of the film were tried and abandoned, scenes reworked, reshoots mounted. Slowly, the symphony took shape. There had been clashes with Warner at every turn. The footage arriving back from Africa made no sense to them. A state of panic was growing, exacerbated by the tales of strife between their stars. The film was delayed, tested, retested, but it is the Miller cut that was finally released on 7 May 2015.

Oh what a lovely day. Vindication must be the greatest of artistic rewards.

Critics were awestruck. *The New York Times* declared it one of the greatest films ever made. Chief critic Manohla Dargis called it her "new *Wizard of Oz*." Fellow filmmakers were drunk was praise. "Oh it's a masterpiece," decreed Quentin Tarantino. "I look at that movie, and I want to quit the business," said Steven

Soderbergh. During a live panel, Gareth Evans was asked to name a recent action scene that had inspired him. Without pausing, he replied, "every frame of *Fury Road*."

The fourth *Mad Max* adventure is a reminder that cinema is a participation sport – not there to be coolly observed like paintings in a gallery, but to flow, to rage, to engulf us in its thrilling fury. There are few films so unrelenting. Perhaps *Alien* and *Aliens*. Or *The Texas Chain Saw Massacre*. Maybe, in a comic mode, how the first three *Indiana Jones* films teeter on the edge of disaster. Maybe *The French Connection* or *The Wages of Fear*, certainly *Mad Max 2*. And, of course, those sublime configurations of calamity in Keaton's universe.

PREVIOUS SPREAD: Furiosa lets rip – in what must have been one of the more cathartic scenes for Theron, her dreams of a Green Space shattered, the road warrior falls to her knees and screams into the uncaring desert. It is one of the most emotionally resonant scenes in the entire saga.

BELOW: Furiosa leaves the War Rig on foot – shot with a dedication to visceral in-camera stunts, *Mad Max: Fury Road* has come to be seen as a great riposte to a CGI-saturated industry.

OPPOSITE: The desert calls to him – Hardy's Max surveys The Wasteland. For Miller the vindication of *Fury Road* was not enough, he will always heed the call of the blighted future.

Yet it is still a very strange film.

Max is slammed around the screen, dangled from bonnets, swung from poles, spitting fuel into pipes, but he remains unreachable, a ghost. He never exactly summons, how does the phrase go: "main character energy." That is left to Theron's Furiosa.

What kind of leader will she make? Aunty Entity was a revolutionary who became a tyrant. Nevertheless, as Max slinks back into the mythical desert, the future does at least look, well, sane. Miller recalled two women coming up to him, on separate continents, one in the USA, one in Australia. They said the same thing: "I've just had a baby girl and I want to call her Furiosa."

"IF I AM GOING TO DIE, I'M GOING TO DIE HISTORIC, ON THE FURY ROAD!"

– NUX

FURIOSA

"THE SURPRISE WAS WHO *WASN'T* BACK – MAD MAX."

The road was jammed with limousines. Beyond the shaded windows, screams pierced the air and flashes strobed concrete. Everywhere the eyes roamed, there were men in black and women in flowing robes. Crowds cried out for the salvation of that rarest of commodities, controlled by the special few – not Aqua-Cola, not guzzaline, but fame. But the traffic crawled along Hollywood Boulevard, bumper to bumper, a fleet of people carriers stocked with nominees. Shiny and chrome. The irony must have made George Miller smile. He had finally slowed down. But that was nothing to the great edifice of irony to which he was headed. The Academy Awards. Mad Max was going to the Oscars. If only Byron Kennedy could see this.

PREVIOUS SPREAD: Taking aim at the future – already smeared in oily war paint, Anya Taylor-Joy as the young Furiosa.

OPPOSITE: An early promotional image portraying Furiosa as a golden idol, in classic George Miller-style – ancient myths mixing with a petrolhead future.

The Dolby Theatre lay at the junction of Hollywood and Highland, a clot of neon and streetlight, currently gilded in crimson carpet and bordered with bleachers, from which fans bayed like a Thunderdome. Five men enter, one man wins. As the great swell of approval that greeted *Mad Max: Fury Road* grew louder and more insistent after its release, an unforeseen and frankly ridiculous notion arose above the din – could Miller's film land the Oscar nominations it so richly deserved, could it even win? Could it overcome the Academy's persistent aversion to genre? Relatively recent victor *The Lord of the Rings*, from over the Tasman Sea, had found the glass

ABOVE: From outsiders to Oscar nominees – *Mad Max: Fury Road* took George Miller and his out-there franchise into the heart of the establishment with ten nominations.

OPPOSITE: South African-born editor Margaret Sixel receives the award for Best Editing. "It was in the edit room the film was finally forged," she said in her speech, with massive understatement.

ceiling hastily repaired in its wake. *Avatar* was a runner-up.

During the long nights of the edit, it became a joke between Margaret Sixel and her husband: "If we don't win an Oscar for this ..." she would rail to the fates. But in that sad, gentle voice, Miller would always remind her this was "not Oscar stuff."

The world saw things differently.

The box-office results read like poetry to Miller. With $380 million, worldwide, it was the hit it needed to be. But there was this lingering doubt that such a figure wasn't quite stratospheric. The glory of *Fury Road* wasn't felt by all. Not immediately. Could it be that the film was good for the masses. These were relative arguments. The existing fan base had found its True North – even minus Mel Gibson. And their ranks were growing by the day. If *Mad Max* was a cult, *Fury Road* was a religion.

Taking a survey of the reviews, they read as if they'd caught a preview of the Second Coming. Words such masterpiece and modern classic are often thrown around like confetti. This was "the Sistine Chapel of action filmmaking," declared Bilge Ebiri in the *Nashville Scene*. Most agreed – this was an expression of cinema at its most exalted. The greatest action movie ever made.

There was bound to be a recalculation of recent history for those who had survived *Fury Road*. The pain came with the ambition. The hardship gave you velocity. Out there everything hurt. You lived *Mad Max*. Then you recovered. And the film made sense of it all.

But their words of acknowledgement came tempered with a shade of weariness like traces of sand still on their tongue.

"It was a pyramid we had to climb," said Zoe Kravitz.

"The fact that it was a huge mess is why it is so brilliant," reflected Abbey Lee.

"We survived; we came out of it. We made something beautiful," said Charlize Theron still sounding like Furiosa.

In May 2015, when their film caught the Cannes Film Festival napping, it was the first time many of the cast had witnessed *Fury Road* in its finished form. A chance to understand where they had been headed under the Namibian sun, all those long months ago. The pieces had come together, and the visual music played like a Doof-Mozart. At the end of the screening there was a silence, like that moment before a collision where time becomes unglued, then the first clap, then a wave, a standing ovation, and finally an outpouring of love.

Hardy made his public apology. With principal cast and crew arrayed along the press conference table like the Last Supper, he turned to Miller. "I have to apologize to you," he began, "because I got frustrated. There was no way that George could have explained what he had conceived."

So, here's the tell. Here's what went down on the night of 28 February 2016, amid the pomp and ceremony of the Dolby Theatre. And it reads like another wrong in a litany of wrongs in the history of the precious Academy. Madness. From ten nominations, *Fury Road* deservedly won Best Editing (how could it not?), Sound Editing, Sound Mixing, Production Design, Costume Design, and Hair and Makeup. A sweep of technicals. Best Picture was lost to crusading journalist drama *Spotlight*.

Most staggering, looking back, is that Miller lost Best Director to *The Revenant*'s master-at-arms, the Mexican Alejandro Gonzalez Iñárritu. That is a category voted for by directors. To be fair, *The Revenant* was a similarly vast and painful undertaking, shot in natural light on the frozen plains of Canada, with Hardy among its number. That was a heavy lead. Maybe Iñárritu was simply a more robust campaigner with a more traditional take on genre, this biting mix of Western and epic. But *Fury Road* was the work of a virtuoso. You came out of it changed. The possibilities of film seemed endless in a way they hadn't since the silent days.

Furthermore, it was relevant. Miller had written a cautionary fable about the political present. This moving metaphor onto which the world could be projected in all its destructive folly: global warming, toxic masculinity, over-exploitation of resources, the jerk toward populism, scaremongering over migration. You name the calamity, and it could be read into the sands of *Fury Road*.

ABOVE: The inbetweener – George Miller's spin on the Arabian Nights idiom, *Three Thousand Years of Longing*, with Tilda Swinton and Idris Elba, was the palate cleanser before *Furiosa* loomed.

That was the power of myth.

From the very beginning, when the blueprint was set down with the rough-hewn *Mad Max*, when Miller had gazed at his fellow countrymen on the nightly news losing it at the parched petrol pumps, there was a message in the mayhem. The madness applied to humankind as a whole.

For reasons beyond anyone's ken, Theron didn't even warrant a nomination for Best Actress. Who even remembers Brie Larson in *Room*, the winner, or Cate Blanchett in *Carol*, Jennifer Lawrence in *Joy*, Charlotte Rampling in *45 Years*, and Saoirse Ronan in *Brooklyn*. All fine performances. But none of them were Furiosa.

Perhaps, this is the *Mad Max* way. To stay on the edge – the loner heading back into the desert. Channelling the punk-provocation of her predecessor Norma Moriceau and their lean future aesthetic, costume designer Jenny Beavan caused a stir with a faux leather jacket, jeans, scarf, and chunky jewellery ensemble. Asked who she was wearing, she replied "Marks & Spencer." She was accused of looking like a "bag lady" at the BAFTAS.

Miller was not dismayed at their defeat. What mattered, he said, was how much "the story means to people." And imagine telling his younger self, mired in the calamity of *Mad Max*, that it would deliver him one day to the Oscars.

In the inverted post-*Fury Road* world, there was now an eagerness for a sequel not seen since *Mad Max 2*. Every interview, every podcast, every talk-show on which Miller played down the goggle-eyed praise, he was asked what comes next. He demurred. He needed a break from the vicissitudes of the desert. He wanted to taste other flavours. But there were ideas, he hinted. Things already imagined during the long grind to get *Fury Road* made.

But now it was Miller who was going to take his time. At last, he would be the master of his own fate. There were raised eyebrows. At seventy-one, he wasn't getting any younger, and these things took their toll, certainly physically. Whatever form it was to take, the sequel would be delayed.

It wasn't simply a matter of refuelling the creative urge. With a familiar ring, the triumph of *Fury Road* briefly turned sour when Miller sued Warner Brothers over unpaid earnings. Studio accounting remains a riddle, wrapped in a mystery, inside a highly dubious idea of what constitutes a profit margin. With a further episode of *Mad Max* in mind, the situation was quietly resolved behind the scenes.

Miller also needed to get another film out of his system. Proof not least to himself that he was more than Max's keeper. Infused with an Arabian Nights mysticism, and based on the A. S. Byatt novella, *Three Thousand Years of Longing* came at those Jungian principles from a different angle. Starring Idris Elba and Tilda Swinton (at one stage it was to be Will Smith and Theron), it was an unconventional if underpowered love story between a contemporary female scholar and a djinn, unleashed from the bottle she buys in an Istanbul bazaar. He then offers her the statutory three wishes. "Spectacular yet fey, it would get any other director thrown out of the pitch meeting and beaten up," wrote Peter Bradshaw in *The Guardian*. Indeed, be careful what you wish for. There are sparks of wit, stories nestled within stories, but it meanders into abstraction, and made next to nothing at the box office.

With a collective sigh of relief, it was back to business. In March 2020, almost five years after *Fury Road*, the announcement came that Miller was at work on his next *Mad Max* symphony. Backed by Warner to the tune of a $168 million (by modern blockbusting

ABOVE: A love story of extreme opposites, Swinton is the stuffy academic who happens upon Elba's disenchanted djinn in an Istanbul bazaar...

LEFT: ... but it would leave audiences and critics cold, barely making a murmur at the box office, another example of how hard to it is to pin Miller down as a director away from the world of *Max*.

ABOVE: Out of the flames – *Furiosa* spans fifteen years of the character's life, explaining how she came to be mixed up with Immortan Joe in the first place.

BELOW: Between a rock and hard place - Furiosa (Anya Taylor-Joy) gets a far-off glimpse of the Citadel, home to Immortan Joe and his War Boys.

OPPOSITE: Having seen her in Edgar Wright's *Last Night in Soho*, George Miller was convinced Taylor-Joy was perfect to play the younger Furiosa, even though she didn't even have a driving licence.

standards a modest outlay), Doug Mitchell returned as producer, Nico Lathouris as co-writer, Colin Gibson as production designer, Sixel as editor, and Beavan on costumes. The surprise was who wasn't back – Mad Max. His relationship with Hardy still uncertain – as well as Hardy's relish for the character – Miller was drawn instead to make a prequel to *Fury Road*, a script that already lay in wait.

Furiosa: A Mad Max Saga would, of course, tell Furiosa's story. As per Miller's synopsis, the pre-prepared script follows a young Furiosa "snatched from the Green Place of Many Mothers". From life stories partially aired in *Fury Road*, Furiosa confesses that her mother lasted only three days, while she fell into the hands of a great biker horde (a nod of the forelock to Toecutter's crew), led by the Warlord Dementus, sweeping through the Wasteland like Genghis Khan (the future mingling with ancient history once more). But standing in his way is the Citadel and a younger Immortan Joe.

The stories cycle and recycle, ending back where they began. Furiosa is another spin on *Yojimbo* (as was *Mad Max 2*) with the young female warrior playing two warlords off against one another. But the idea of two despots was new, two toxic tyrants coming to blows, a war film no less. And a character study: Furiosa will be learning her skills at the wheel, learning to survive, learning to hate, while losing her arm, and losing her soul.

"Again, it's uniquely familiar," teased Miller. "And probably the biggest difference is the timespan. *Fury Road* happened over three days and two nights and this one happens over fifteen

"FOR THE LONGEST TIME, I THOUGHT WE COULD JUST USE CG DE-AGING ON CHARLIZE."

– GEORGE MILLER

ABOVE: A hard act to follow – recapturing Charlize Theron's performance as Furiosa is a tall order, but the prequel offers a completely different, younger side to the character.

OPPOSITE TOP: Chris Hemsworth as Warlord Dementus – the flamboyant new villain, equal parts charisma and insanity – offered the A-lister a chance to ruffle up his heroic image.

OPPOSITE: Maxian motifs – Furiosa emerges from a dusty burial, just as Tom Hardy's Max does in *Fury Road*.

years. So, it's a *saga*. This is the story of all the people in the Wasteland, seen through the experience of Furiosa."

Questions, questions. How will a *Mad Max* film bear the weight of so much time? Even *Thunderdome*, the most epic in construction, was still measured in days, not years. This is a distinct shift in idiom – all the previous film were, as Miller said, told "on the run". How will it bear the weight of so much expectation. How do you ever follow *Fury Road*?

To start with, by getting back to basics. Miller was heading home. Back to futures past – not only *Furiosa's* backstory, but Max's, and his own. On 20 May 2022, they reconvened in Broken Hill, the landscape unchanged and uncaring, the first *Mad Max* film to travel old roads. Back in Australia, where the locals have heard it all before: Broken Hill, Silverton, Mundi-Mundi, plus the old Fox Studios in Sydney, now in the hands of Disney.

An old location, then, but with a new cast. Local A-lister Chris Hemsworth, his figure as bounteously muscled as Lord Humungus, was a surprise enlistee. He and Miller had met as a courtesy and fallen in love. Caught on a red carpet, shortly after the news broke, the erstwhile Thor blurted that it was a "dream" to join a *Mad Max* film. It was a national heritage. The pretty boy from Melbourne had made his name with heroics (*Star Trek, Rush, Blackhat, Extraction*), only this time he was bad to the bone. It was mad enough to work.

In describing Dementus, Hemsworth chose his words carefully. "He's a very complicated, somewhat evil individual... Yeah, you don't believe you're evil though. I'm saying that from the outset, I found ways to defend his actions and empathize and understand him as I had to. That was my job."

Warlord Dementus, like Lord Humungus, Aunty Entity, and Immortan Joe, is a product of his environment. "He's been birthed into a space where it's kill or be killed," he insisted. All this medieval futurism, the old-new, is bound to lead to a little insanity.

As for the look: leather pants, cavalry waistcoat, codpiece, long dark locks, prosthetic nose, and piratical beard. Plus a bugle. And a tiny stolen teddy bear (a gesture perhaps to the lost children of *Thunderdome*?). He has the aura of Captain Hook. And a "manipulative charisma," concluded the actor: another demagogue delighted by the sound of his own voice.

Hemsworth described a shoot getting back in touch with its inner biker, and the oil smudged borderline between fact and fiction of the original *Mad Max*. When it came to his horde, a lot of the cast were, well, "ex-criminals". One was a bona fide Hell's Angel. They were, he said happily, "people from very colourful, interesting, complicated lives".

During casting, Miller got up to his old tricks. He would invite all these oddballs from the fringes of society in for a chat, asking them to tell him a story about themselves. They would really open up. "He said that all of a sudden, there was such a truth there, that they had been seen for the first time," explained Hemsworth. "Someone hadn't pushed them aside and said, 'Well, you've messed up, you're finished'. They were given a second chance. There was a redemption quality to it."

"*FURY ROAD* HAPPENED OVER THREE DAYS AND TWO NIGHTS AND THIS ONE HAPPENS OVER FIFTEEN YEARS. SO, IT'S A SAGA."

– GEORGE MILLER

PREVIOUS SPREAD: A window on the soul – as with Charlize Theron's version of the character, so much of Furiosa's powder keg of emotion is conveyed through Anya Taylor-Joy's huge eyes.

ABOVE: Master of ceremonies – Warlord Dementus starts the engines of his racers in the distinctive style of Dr. Dealgood (Edwin Hodgeman) from *Mad Max Beyond Thunderdome.*

As it was with Toecutter's gang, Dementus gained absolute dedication from his soldiers. Rain or shine, cooking under that scalding Maxian sun; through the cornucopia of complexities that still come with this heathen world, whatever the technological advances in putting the fury inside a camera; they were there, ready to follow him in to battle.

"Thick or thin, they're showing up," grinned Hemsworth.

Working with Miller has lived up to its own mythology. All those plangent tales from behind the scenes of Max's past. The elusive visionary, his mind a conveyer belt of arcane action, under pressure to outdo his last standing rival – himself, or the younger version of himself.

Hemsworth, arriving on set better equipped for Miller's method than previous stars, found the long shoot exhausting, but exhausting in the best way. He relished how every single frame was thought out. Every frame was necessary for the desired effect. Every frame was essential in shaping character and narrative. What Hemsworth called, "the grander plan".

In November 2021, British actor Tom Burke (who had played Orson Welles in *Mank*) was announced in a significant mystery role. In early footage, he can be spotted with his forehead pressed to Furiosa, in a clinch. There will be more to this role, a trajectory, even a transformation, which will add to her bitterness.

A degree of continuity was maintained with the return of Nathan Jones as Rictus Erectus, the walking tumescence, and Angus Sampson

as The Organic Mechanic, the nearest thing the Citadel's makeshift society has to a practising doctor (a former life in medicine is assumed – he knows his way around a blood transfusion). The mythos has him sewing up wounds by plucking hairs from this patchy scalp.

"There is a scene in it where all the bad guys drive off after the amputee ..." said Sampson, recalling scenes that were cut from *Fury Road*, and dropping hints that Furiosa's missing appendage was the result of one of his medical procedures. "As the 44 cars drove off chasing Max and the girls, the dust cleared to reveal my character, The Organic Mechanic, doing something disgusting."

He was basically defecating in the desert.

The Organic Mechanic, preoccupied by the specifics of his profession – he has the same prophet-of-doom air as the camshaft and brake-pad mechanics of previous films – is undoubtedly a cypher for Doctor Miller. And maybe, just maybe there is some vision of Max. Remember that Interceptor seen on set. What could it portend? Pushed on the whereabouts of the antihero, Miller admitted that "Max was lurking around somewhere in this story".

The other startling absentee was Theron.

"For the longest time, I thought we could just use CG de-aging on Charlize," said Miller. Filmed at roughly the same time, Harrison Ford shed forty years for the opening sequence of *Indiana Jones and the Dial of Destiny*. But that presented Miller's prequel with a digital crutch – a frame-by-frame CGI glaze that might eat into

ABOVE: Past lives – Furiosa shares a rare intimate moment with a fellow road warrior (Tom Burke).

ABOVE: All shiny and chrome – in time-honoured tradition, Warlord Dementus's biker gang attack a tanker protected by a battalion of War Boys.

OPPOSITE TOP: Getting medieval – the younger Furiosa brings down a refinery portcullis in another explosive situation.

OPPOSITE: Warlord Dementus (centre) leads his hoards into battle – the return of a biker gang pays tribute to Toecutter and his cronies from the original *Mad Max*. The flying bike (front) is more in keeping with the gyrocopter of *Mad Max 2*.

the in-camera prowess that was the doctrine of *Mad Max*ing. As well as eat into the budget. More pertinently, was the technology really up to it? "I don't think we're there yet," he admitted. One dystopian venue *Furiosa* didn't want to visit was the Uncanny Valley.

The calculus became simple. He would cast a younger variation of the part. It had worked with Max, so why not the iconic Furiosa?

That was tough for Theron to swallow. She had been through hell with that character. Watching someone else fill her boots was going to be heart-breaking, but she remained politic in her remarks.

"Listen, I fully respect George, if not more so in the aftermath of making *Fury Road* with him. He's a master, and I wish him nothing but the best... I really love that character, and I'm so grateful that I had a small part in creating her."

Jodie Comer was mentioned, someone is always mentioned, but once Miller met Anya

Taylor-Joy, he didn't look back. Edgar Wright had shown him *Last Night in Soho* and arranged for them to meet.

Taylor-Joy was exotic. Born in Zambia to a Scottish father and Spanish-English mother, a diplomat and a psychologist respectively, she was raised in Argentina and London. Her wide-wide eyes and striking features landed her modelling jobs, before a breakthrough in *The Witch*. She could mix vulnerability with dark currents. *Split, The New Mutants, The Northman* and the smash television hit *The Queen's Gambit* established her in the short-sighted eyes of studios.

When it came to an audition, Miller had her read the "I'm as mad as hell" speech from *Network*. Peter Finch at his wits' end. It was a good piece, he thought, almost a monologue, and full of vim. He had used it before in his casting games. This was the same speech on which Lee went full preacher to land the role of The Dag for *Fury Road*. Under different circumstances, an alternate timeline, Lee would have been a prospective Furiosa. Miller filmed it on his iPhone and sent it to the studio. This is my young Furiosa. Warner didn't need persuading.

"I am going to work so hard at this," she promised. To push beyond her limits. Deliberately, she didn't meet Theron until after filming wrapped on 12 October 2022.

PREVIOUS SPREAD: The shape of things to come – Furiosa defends the rig from enemy assault. In this case, with the help of a giant harpoon.

ABOVE: The mask fits – Furiosa will also explain how the despicable Immortan Joe came to rule the Citadel ...

OPPOSITE: ... and how the road warrior queen will gain that iconic look: shaved head, oil smear, and a mechanical prosthetic instead of a left arm. This is the legend within the legend of *Mad Max*.

In the flush of landing the role of a lifetime, Taylor-Joy said that she was quite happy to shave her long blonde hair. But Beavan, Oscar in her handbag, hinted that Miller had a different look in store for the younger Furiosa.

There was one slight issue – Taylor-Joy couldn't drive. She didn't have a licence. Miller smiled. Where she was going that didn't really matter. He had a get out of jail free card.

It is early 2024, and the legend can be felt rumbling on the horizon once more: cars, twisted into new-fangled shapes; drivers in leather and metal, pirates of the hot plains; a heroine, scarred by experience, turned a road warrior, maybe mad.

Miller and Sixel are deep in the maze of their edit, despair mingling with confidence. The images unfolding before them. The camera slung inches above the road. He reaches once more for the film that lies under his skin.

Footage is released, a nitro-charged tease of the next stage of evolution. Hints of storylines, motifs, themes, stunts, and the oily pot pouri of established mythology. "A lot of the film will be familiar," hinted Miller," but a lot of it will be new." Women on foot and on horseback even, fleeing through the Green Place, is the first sighting of living trees since *Mad Max*. Furiosa reborn out of a dusty burial, just as Max will be one day. A refinery as huge as CGI can make it, towering over the highway like the Emerald City in Oz. A propellor-lifted bike recalling the gyrocopter of yesteryear. The unmistakable figure of Immortan Joe, younger but nevertheless drawing on a respirator, his hair ash blonde. Dementus in his motorized chariot, cape fluttering, like *Ben-hur*, or *Thor*. A tanker, maybe the War Rig itself, all shiny and chrome (and inlaid with carvings of Dementus), under fire from a swarm of bikers.

Visual rock 'n' roll.

SOURCES

WEBSITES

All box office figures come via Boxofficemojo.com

Variety.com

Mad Max Garage Inc "I'm just here for the gasoline" Facebook group

MAGAZINES, NEWSPAPERS AND ONLINE ARTICLES

Barra, Allen, *"Nostalgic for the Apocalypse": George Miller's Long, Strange Trip to Mad Max Fury Road, Salon*, 14 May 2015

Billson, Anne, *George Miller Talks About Mad Max, Heroes, & Tina Turner: The 1985 Interview, Time Out*, October 1985

Bowen, Chuck, *Blu-ray Review: George Miller's Mad Max Trilogy on Warner Home Video, Slant Magazine*, 5 June 2013

Brooks, Xan, *"We're Hardwired for Stories": Mad Max Director George Miller on Myths, Medicine, and a Pointy-Eared Idris Elba, The Guardian*, 18 August 2022

Buchanan, Kyle, *Furiosa's Back: George Miller Discusses the Next Mad Max Movie, New York Times*, 14 May 2020

Buchanan, Kyle, *"It Was Horrible": Inside Charlize Theron and Tom Hardy's Mad Max Feud*, *Vanity Fair*, 22 February 2022

Buckmaster, Luke, *"It's Absolutely Disgusting": Watching George Miller's Rarely Seen First Film, The Guardian*, 15 August 2022

Chute, David, *The Ayatollah of the Moviola, Film Comment*, July/August 1982

Collins, Eve, *The Entire Mad Max Timeline Explained, Looper*, 4 January 2021

Conterio, Martyn, *Mad Max: Beyond Thunderdome at 35: Remembering Tina Turner's Ruthless Villain Aunty Entity, NME*, 10 July 2020

Conterio, Martyn, *Throwback: Mad Max, Sci-fi Now*, 7 January 2021

Corliss, Richard, *Apocalypse… Pow!, Time*, 1982

Cumbow, Robert C., *Simmer of '85: Mad Max: Beyond Thunderdome at 25, Slant Magazine*, 19 July 2010

Davids, Bryan, *Charlize Theron on The Old Guard and Her Heartbreak Over the Furiosa Prequel, Hollywood Reporter*, 6 July 2020

Fuge, Jonathan, *Furiosa: A Mad Max Saga Releases Epic New Poster; Chris Hemsworth Praises Director George Miller's Vision, Movieweb,* 11 December 2023

Grobel, Lawrence, *Mel Gibson Interview, Playboy*, July 1995

Gunning, Cathal, *How an Australian Cult Thriller Inspired Mad Max, Screen Rant,* 1 May 2021

Harris, Rachel Lee, *Behind the Makeup and Costumes of Fury Road, The New York Times,* 10 February 2016

Hill, Logan, *Mad Max: Fury Road's Sunt Guy Went Out with an Epic Bang, Wired,* 17 May 2016

Hill, Logan, *Mad Max: What It Takes to Make the Most Intense Movie Ever, Wired*, 11 May 2015

Horwell, Veronica, *Norma Moriceau Obituary, The Guardian*, 14 September 2016

Kaufman, Tina and Page, Peter, *Mad Max: Another Rider of the Silver Screen, Filmnews (Sydney NSW)*, 1 July 1979

Lambert, Harper, *Furiosa: Chris Hemsworth Announces Start of Filming on Mad Max: Fury Road Prequel*, The Wrap, 1 June 2020

Lane, Anthony, *High Gear – Mad Max: Fury Road, The New Yorker*, 15 May 2015

Lattanzio, Ryan, *Fury Road Prequel Furiosa Delayed One Year, Sets New 2024 Release, Indiewire*, 10 September 2021

Loder, Kurt, *Mad Max: The Heroes of Thunderdome, Rolling Stone*, 29 August 1985

Lofficier, Jean-March and Randy, *A Few Days on the Set of Mad Max III Beyond Thunderdome, Starlog*, June 1985

Looper staff, *Mad Max: Fury Road Scenes We Never Got to See, Looper*, 29 January 2021

Lyttelton, Oliver, *5 Things You Might Not Know About Mad Max, IndieWire*, 12 April 2012

MacInnes, Paul, *George Miller: "The Last Thing I Wanted to do was Another Mad Max movie, The Guardian*, 2 October 2015

McCausland, James, *Scientists' Warnings Unheeded, The Courier Mail*, 4 December 2006

McGovern, Joe, *Mad Max: Mel Gibson Talks George Miller in Thunderdome Interview, via Entertainment Weekly*, 1985

McGuire, Kay, *Mad Max: Furiosa's Origins & Backstory Before Fury Road Explained, Screen Rant*, October 2020

Nordine, Michael, *Mad Max Beyond Thunderdome Making of Shows How*

George Miller & Mel Gibson Created the Classic, IndieWire, 5 June 2016

Northrup, Ryan, *Chris Hemsworth Hints at His Mystery Villain Role in Furiosa, Screen Rant,* 18 November 2022

Oganesyan, Natalie, *Furiosa Cast, Release Date and Everything We Know About the Mad Max: Fury Road Prequel, The Wrap,* 29 May 2020

Peres, Daniel, *Tom Hardy Lets His Guard Down, GQ*, 21 April 2015

Polowy, Kevin, *Meet iOTA, the Guitar Hero from Mad Max: Fury Road, Yahoo! Entertainment*, 19 May 2015

Raddish, Christina, *Writer/Director George Miller Talks Mad Max: Fury Road, Returning to the Post-Apocalyptic World, Thousands of Storyboards, and More at Comic-Con, Collider*, 1 August 2014

Rich, Katy, *Mad Max: Fury Road Director George Miller: "I Can't Help But Be a Feminist", Vanity Fair*, 14 May 2015

Sternbergh, Adam, *Mad Max: Fury Road Director George Miller on His unlikely Oscar Contender and Even Unlikelier Career, Vulture*, 12 February 2016

Tucker, Reed, *Mad Max Creator: Why I Cut Mel Gibson from Fury Road, New York Post*, 9 May 2015

Unattributed, *Mad Max: Beyond Thunderdome, Sounds*, 23 November 1985

Unattributed, *Catching Up with the Feral Kid: A Chat with Emil Minty, NateWatchesCoolMovies,* 5 September 2015

Unattributed, *George Miller An Unlikely Director of Mad Max II, Chicago Sun-Times*, 8 September 1982

Unattributed, *Stunt Driver Phil Brock on Mad Max, Frenchman's Farm and Brother Peter, Cult Film Alley*, 27 July 2019

Unattributed, *A Tribute to Byron Kennedy, Filmnews (Sydney NSW),* 1 July 1983

Utichi, Joe, *Inside George Miller's 20-Year Quest to Make Three Thousand Years of Longing, as Furiosa Revs Her Engines – Cannes, Deadline*, 17 May 2022

Welsh, Daniel, *Oscars 2016: Jenny Bevan Could Not Care Less What You Think of Her Outfit, The Huffington Post*, 29 February 2016

DOCUMENTARIES AND PODCASTS

Behind the Scenes – Mad Max: Fury Road, Warner Home Video, 2015

Furiosa Returns? George Miller on the Next Mad Max, Five Years of Fury Road and Heath Ledger as Max, Popverse, via YouTube, 15 August 2020

George Miller: Australian Screen, an NFSA Website, Undated

George Miller - Mad Max Fury Road Interview with Richard Crouse, In Isolation with Richard Crouse, via *YouTube*, 4 May 2015

George Miller on Tina Turner, ABC News Australia, May 25 2023

Going Mad: The Battle of Fury Road, Warner Bros. Entertainment, 2020

Mad Max: Fury Road Interview – Charlize Theron, Rotten Tomatoes, 2015

The Madness of Max, Warner Home Video, 2015

The Making of Mad Max: Fury Road, Warner Home Video, 2015

The Making of Mad Max: Beyond Thunderdome, Warner Home Video, 2015

Mel Gibson and George Miller interview, The Bobbie Wygant Archive, via YouTube, 1985

Road War: The Making of Mad Max 2, Warner Home Video, 2015

Special – Mad Max, London Weekend Television, via YouTube, 15 March 1986

Terry Hayes Interview, Mr. Media, via YouTube, May 2014

The Story of the Mad Max Interceptor, MFP – Map Film Productions, 2019

BIBLIOGRAPHY

Bernstein, Abbey, *The Art of Mad Max: Fury Road*, Titan Books, 15 May 2015

Buckmaster, Luke, *Miller and Max: George Miller and the Making of a Film Legend,* Hardie Grant Books, 2017

Buchanan, Kyle, *Blood, Sweat, & Chrome*, William Morrow, 2022

Conterio, Martyn, *Constellations: Mad Max*, Auteur, 2019

ACKNOWLEDGEMENTS

I can still remember the first time I ventured into the blasted future. My entry point was *Mad Max 2,* watched illicitly on VHS, a rite of passage back then. Somewhere in the mid-eighties. Only since have I come to see how important all these films are in demonstrating the potential of action cinema – and therefore the potential of cinema as a whole. They are as vital as the works of Chaplin and Keaton; as inventive and ambitious as the anything by DeMille, Kurosawa, Spielberg, or Cameron; as strange and funny and as non-conformist as anything by Buñuel, Tarkovsky, or Lynch. There is a hyper-lyricism at work here that could only come out of Australia. On first viewing, however, it was simply about awakening to how dark and thrilling films could be. And how damn cool. I loved how the duped and defeated Max laughs at the end. I still do.

George Miller is an auteur by stealth. He doesn't conform to any club's rules. He doesn't play the artist. But he is one. The great Ayatollah of Visual Rock'n'rolla. No one else could have made these films. There is something uncanny about their creation, the ability (often against great odds and desperate conditions) to assemble poetry out of a blizzard. Genius is a mystery, and his peers look upon his *Mad Max* films almost as artefacts of some alien civilisation. Something beyond their ken. I am reminded of an interview I did shortly after *Fury Road* opened in 2015 entirely unrelated - with the late, hugely lamented Jonathan Demme, a magnificent director in his own right. Before I had uttered a word, he exclaimed, "Ian, have you seen *FURY ROAD*? Have you seen it? OH MY GOD. What a movie..." It took a while to get him on topic. All else had been rendered irrelevant by the joy of experiencing that film.

All these films, from their humblest, riskiest origins to the head-spinning brilliance of *Fury Road* are legend. And indeed built upon deep-rooted concepts of a mythology that runs through the history of mankind. The idea of story as something primal and wonderful.

Too often dismissed as genre, it struck me that the world of *Mad Max* has been neglected in terms of serious film writing. Nonetheless, it was such a pleasure to discover an underground of appreciation in the darker recesses of YouTube and Facebook, and to explore the subculture that has grown up around the quartet (soon to be quintet) of rock'n'roll collisions. And to absorb the marvellous writing that has come out of these films – especially *Fury Road*.

And what a joy they were to write about. There is something in these films, not just the frenetic stunts, but the sheer personality that accelerates the prose and stirs the imagination. What you have in your hands is a history of a darkly imagined future, a celebration of moviemaking at its most tangible, and a biography, in part, of Miller and his long-lost partner Byron Kennedy. It is also a book about Australia and the movies this complex country has birthed.

My thanks go to the gang, for the support and wisdom that goes way back: Steve Hornby, Dave Hobbs, Ian Freer, Mark Dining, Phil Wilding, Dan Jolin, Adam Smith, Liz Moody, and more recently Robin Block. And, even if he may not remember, to Ben Elsdon, who shared that first viewing of *Mad Max 2*. Once again, I have benefitted immeasurably from the guidance and patience of my editor, Robert Nichols, at Palazzo, and the expert eye of my copy editor David Inglesfield. And I can happily report that, at the very least, the book is a visual triumph to match the Miller aesthetic, which is down to Martin Stiff at Amazing15 design.

Finally, this book is dedicated to Wai Hui, who is Furiosa-cool and my true inspiration in everything.

Picture Credits
T: Top; B: Bottom; L: Left; R: Right

Courtesy of Alamy:
20th Century Fox/Pictorial Press 22; Album/Village Roadshow 138, 145, 146B, 150, 160, 161, 167, 178; Album/Warner Bros 68, 84, 89, 99, 106, 122; Allstar Picture Library/Warner Bros 42, 44B, 52, 61, 117; Allstar Picture Library 27; BFA 129B; BFA/Warner Bros 65, 98; CASBAH/IGOR/Album 23; Cinematic/Warner Bros 41, 44T, 80, 102T; Collection Christophel/Algonquin 129T; Collection Christophel/Warner Bros 13, 49T, 93, 94; Everett Collection Inc 32; Globe Photos/Zuma Press Inc 134; Heritage Image Partnership Ltd 30; Hilke Maunder 9; Ingo Oeland 19; Jasin Boland/Village Roadshow/Photo 12, 147, 152, 164, 166; Jim Ruymen/UPI 172; Landmark Media/Warner Bros 96, 103, 110T, 110B, 113B, 114T, 119, 121, 169, 176T, 176B, 177, 179B, 180, 182, 183, 184, 185T, 185B, 186, 188, 189; Metro Goldwyn Mayer/Album 174; Metro Goldwyn Mayer/BFA 175B; Metro Goldwyn Mayer/PictureLux/The Hollywood Archive 175T; Moviestore Collection 31, 132; Moviestore/Warner Bros 90; Photo 12/Warner Bros 39B, 40, 46B, 71, 77B, 85B, 86, 91; Photo 12/Warner Bros 6; Pictorial Press/Warner Bros 36, 60; PictureLux/The Hollywood Archive 173; PictureLux/The Hollywood Archive/Universal Pictures 128, 130; PictureLux/The Hollywood Archive/Warner Bros 51, 136, 156; Prod DB © Golden Harvest 46T; ScreenProd/Photononstop/Warner Bros 14, 115B; TCD/Prod. DB/Kennedy Miller Prods 62, 64, 66, 70, 73, 75, 76, 85T, 87, 92, 100, 101B, 120, 123, 131; TCD/Prod.DB/Kennedy Miller Prods/Village Roadshow/Warner Bros 139, 142T, 142B, 143T, 144, 148, 151, 154, 157B, 158, 159, 162, 163; TCD/Prod.DB/The Film House 26; TCD/Prod.DB/Warner Bros Cover, 10, 11T, 12, 16, 34, 38, 45, 55, 56, 58, 82, 171, 179T; United Archives GmbH 28, 29; United Archives GmbH/Warner Bros 67, 74, 112, 114B, 116; Village Roadshow Pictures/Entertainment Pictures170; Village Roadshow/Album 21; Warner Bros/Everett Collection 24, 101T; Xavier Durand 127; Zuma Press Inc 124

Courtesy of Rex Shutterstock:
Aip-Filmways/Kobal/Warner Bros 37; American Int/Everett/Warner Bros 11b; Jasin Boland/Village Roadshow/Kobal 141, 146T, 157T; Kennedy Miller Prods/Kobal 43, 48, 49B, 54, 59; Moviestore/Warner Bros 39T, 104, 105, 107, 108, 111, 113T, 115T, 118; Snap/Kennedy Miller Prods 95; Village Roadshow/Kobal 140, 155; Warner Bros/Everett 15; Warner Bros/Kobal 77T, 78, 81, 88, 102B

Courtesy of Getty Images:
Ross Anthony Willis/Fairfax Media 26